TO

Alan Schmitt
2018

The Will of God Is...

ALAN SCHMITT

Copyright © 2014 Alan Schmitt.

All rights reserved. No part of this book may be used or reproduced by any means, graphic, electronic, or mechanical, including photocopying, recording, taping or by any information storage retrieval system without the written permission of the publisher except in the case of brief quotations embodied in critical articles and reviews.

Scripture taken from the New King James Version. Copyright 1979, 1980, 1982 by Thomas Nelson, inc. Used by permission. All rights reserved.

WestBow Press books may be ordered through
booksellers or by contacting:

WestBow Press
A Division of Thomas Nelson & Zondervan
1663 Liberty Drive
Bloomington, IN 47403
www.westbowpress.com
1 (866) 928-1240

Because of the dynamic nature of the Internet, any web addresses or links contained in this book may have changed since publication and may no longer be valid. The views expressed in this work are solely those of the author and do not necessarily reflect the views of the publisher, and the publisher hereby disclaims any responsibility for them.

Any people depicted in stock imagery provided by Thinkstock are models, and such images are being used for illustrative purposes only.
Certain stock imagery © Thinkstock.

ISBN: 978-1-4908-2596-0 (sc)
ISBN: 978-1-4908-2595-3 (e)

Library of Congress Control Number: 2014902572

Printed in the United States of America.

WestBow Press rev. date: 02/05/2014

Contents

Preface: A Journey through the Fog vii

Chapter 1: The Will of God is Desire & Design ... 1
Chapter 2: Two Other Wills 9
Chapter 3: The Grace Package 17
Chapter 4: The Will of God is… No other gods! 23
Chapter 5: The Will of God is… Don't Abuse My Name! 28
Chapter 6: The Will of God is… Go to Church! 35
Chapter 7: The Will of God is… Family! 43
Chapter 8: The Will of God is… Be a Lover, not a Fighter! 50
Chapter 9: The Will of God is… Look the Other Way! 59
Chapter 10: The Will of God is… Don't Steal Anything! 67
Chapter 11: The Will of God is… Let Your Yes be Yes and Your No be No! 75
Chapter 12: The Will of God is… Don't Let What Others Have, Get in the Way of What you have! 84

Epilogue: The Will of God is… God's Will or My Will? An interview with God 93

Preface

A Journey through the Fog

It was Christmas Day, 1968. My wife and I were married three months earlier in October. I was serving in the United State Air Force, stationed at Dyess Air Force Base, Abilene, TX. Because of the two-week leave I took for the wedding and honeymoon, we resolved ourselves to the reality that we would be spending our first Christmas together in Texas, rather than with family back home in Missouri. We put up one of those gaudy aluminum trees that were popular in the 1960's and mailed all our presents for family home to Missouri.

When I checked the duty roster for the week of December 23, I discovered that I had Christmas Eve and Christmas day off. Young and foolish as we were, my wife and I decided to make a whirlwind trip home for Christmas. We would leave after work on the 23rd and make it home in time for breakfast on the 24th. We would then leave Christmas day about 10:00 pm and drive all night so I could be back for work on Thursday. We had a plan!

Our plan was right on schedule until we crossed the Missouri-Oklahoma state line on Christmas night. About five miles into Oklahoma, we hit a wall of fog that was so thick visibility was, at best, about eight feet! For the next three hours, we drove twenty-miles an hour taking turns driving and leaning out the window to make sure we were still on the road. But by the grace of God, we made it home safely and I reported to work on time.

My purpose for sharing our 1968 Christmas night adventure is because it reminds me of another adventure I have been on. The adventure of my personal journey to discover what the Will of God is: A journey that has taken me through a thick fog of unanswered questions.

Is God's Will simply what God wants me to do? Okay. What does God want me to do? How do I find out what God wants me to do? How do I know I am doing what God wants me to do? How do we know if something that happens to us, our community, or the world is God's Will? Are catastrophic events the Will of God? Does He cause them? Why doesn't He prevent them? Is it God's Will that bad things happen to good people? Is it God's Will that people suffer? Does God cause every thing that happens, to happen? Why does God heal some people and not others? Why is knowing God's Will so complicated and elusive? Why is trying to figure out God's Will sometimes like driving through thick fog in the middle of the night?

Over the past thirty-five years, I have discovered that I am not alone in my journey. As a local pastor, I have been called upon to answer a vast assortment of questions about the Will of God. In times of personal and family crisis, debilitating emotional pain, and the grief of personal loss, I have been called upon to discern, decipher, and defend the Will of God. I have found that to be a difficult task many times, in part, because of my own struggle to understand the Will of God for my life.

Consequently, armed with a Bible as my road map and the Holy Spirit as my compass, I set out on a journey to discover what the Will of God is. My journey has taken me to places in scripture I have never been before, it has revealed things to me that I have never seen before, and it has challenged my understanding of the Will of God in ways I could never have imagined. While my journey has been disorienting at times, I have tried to remain faithful to my biblical map and my Spiritual guide.

Hopefully, I have been headed in the right direction, because in the pages that follow, I invite you to join me on my journey of discovery and discernment of the Will of God.

Before we move on the next chapter, I want to acknowledge the work of Michael Bronson. In his book, *Finding the Elusive Will of God*, I have found four invaluable insights that have helped me gain a new perspective on understanding the Will of God.

Bronson proposes, "There are four main reasons why we may not understand God's dealings with us. First, because we are finite creatures, our perception of God is usually distorted. Second, true spiritual growth usually involves difficulties, challenges, and times of testing. Third, God uses 'impossible' circumstances to prove Himself to you and to the world. Fourth, God, for whatever reason, has chosen to let certain aspects of Himself remain a mystery to us."[1]

Thank You

No one writes a book alone. Most of the printed words may come from the one whose name appears on the cover. But the inspiration, insights, and experiences that produce those printed words come from a wonderful circle of family, friends, collogues, and all those unnamed or forgotten saints that God so graciously plants along our life journey. This book is no exception.

To those who have been a source of inspiration to me, those who have graciously shared their insights with me, and to those whose experiences have illuminated the path of my life journey, I say *Thank You*!

I am especially indebted to those who have devoted many hours to reading my words, proofing my words, and offering invaluable advice and counsel regarding how I could better put my words together. To each of you, I say *Thank You*!

While on the *References* page I have attempted to give credit to specific works I have used in my "Will of God" journey, I accept the reality that time and fading memory have inadvertently caused me to forget others. To all who may fall into this category, I say *Thank You!*

Finally, I offer my eternal gratitude to the gracious God who has bestowed on me the honor of using my words, to speak His word.

In the name of the Father, and of the Son, and of the Holy Spirit: Amen!

Alan Schmitt
2013

One

The Will of God is Desire & Design

Let's begin our Will of God journey with a biblical understanding of the word "will." Will is desire and design. What someone wants to happen, when they want it to happen, how they want it to happen, and what they want the results to be.

Common biblical synonyms or descriptor words for will include wish, would, desire, choice, request, require, command, and decree. Here's an example from Luke 2:2-3: *"In those days Caesar Augustus issued a decree that a census should be taken of the entire Roman world."* (desire) *"And everyone went to his own town to register."* (design)

When we hear the word "will", we often think of the other kind of will: a legal declaration of how a person wishes their possessions to be disposed of after their death. The scripture addresses it as well. It is interesting to note that no written Israelite wills existed until the first century B.C. They were unnecessary because of the strict inheritance customs of the Hebrew people.

While this use of the word "will" applies more to relationships between members of a family rather than the relationship between humankind and God, the elements of desire and design are present. Numbers 27:8-11: (design) *"Say to the Israelites, 'If a man dies and leaves no son, turn his inheritance over to his daughter. If he has no daughter, give his inheritance to his brothers. If he has no brothers, give his inheritance to his father's brothers. If his father had no brothers, give his inheritance to the nearest relative in his clan, that he may possess it.* (desire) *This is to be a legal requirement for the Israelites, as the Lord commanded Moses.'"*

When the biblical understanding of will as desire and design is applied to God, we are able to establish a working definition of the Will of God as the desire and design of God. The biblical writers refine our working definition with two descriptors:

1. The desire of God as understood to be the predestined Will of God.
2. The design of God as understood to be the sovereign Will of God. In this chapter, I want to direct our focus on the sovereign Will of God.

The sovereign Will of God means God has the ultimate authority to do whatever God wants to do, however God wants to do it, whenever God wants to do it. We can see this understanding reflected in 1 Chronicles 29:11-13 when we hear David say; *"Yours, O LORD, is the greatness and the power and the glory and the majesty and the splendor, for everything in heaven and earth is yours. Yours, O LORD, is the kingdom; you are exalted as head over all. Wealth and honor come from you; you are the ruler of all things. In your hands are strength and power to exalt and give strength to all. Now, our God, we give you thanks, and praise your glorious name."*

Does that passage sound familiar? How about if I said it this way: *For Thine is the kingdom, and the power, and the glory forever. Amen.* Do you think it is a mere coincidence that the sovereign Will of God is proclaimed at the end of a universal prayer in which we pray, *Your will be done on earth as it is in heaven?*

In early cultures, the sovereign Will of God was most evidenced in the natural order of things. When humankind observed and experienced the natural world, there was an inherent desire to know why things happened or what caused them to happen. If they could figure that out, they might be able to better survive, prepare for, prevent, or even control the events of the natural world.

When they attempted to understand the natural world by comparing the unknown of nature to the known of their cultural structure, they began to see a cause-effect relationship. They reasoned that nothing happened without something or someone causing it to happen. When they would experience catastrophic events in nature, they would conclude that the only thing powerful enough to cause them had to be one or more divine beings. Since a division of labor was common place in each culture, they reasoned that it must be the same in the heavenly realm; so the belief in polytheism, the belief in many gods, was born.

From this early cause-effect observation there evolved the belief that if bad things happened, that must mean the god's were angry. If good things happened, the gods were happy. So, it was in the best interest of humankind to figure out how to keep the gods happy. That is, to figure out what the will of the gods was and develop a system of practices designed to keep them happy.

The tradition that emerged from the history of the Israelites followed the same path of reasoning with one exception. They believed there was only one god in charge of it all, the God *Yahweh*. A belief system that was based on two of the first three commandments:

1. Exodus 20:3: "*You shall have no other gods before me.*" It is important to note that the Hebrew word for *before me* can also mean *beside me.* What that means is that you shall not believe in any other god as being more

sovereign than me, nor are you to believe in any other god as being equal to me.
2. Exodus 20:4: *"You shall not make for yourself an idol in the form of anything in heaven above or on the earth beneath or in the waters below."* Not only will you not believe in any other divine god, you shall not create or be subject to any man-made god. From those commandments, there evolved a complex system of *Mitzvah* (commandments) designed to keep Yahweh happy. There are 613 Mitzvah.

The Old Testament understanding of the relationship between God and humankind is based on covenants, an agreement between two people or two groups that involve promises on the part of each to the other. The concept of covenant between God and His people is one of the most important theological truths of the Bible.

By making a covenant with Abram, God promised to bless his descendants and to make them His special people. Abram, in return, was to remain faithful to God and to serve as a channel through which God's blessings could flow to the rest of the world. Genesis 12:1-3: *"The Lord said to Abram, 'Leave your country, your people and your father's household and go to the land I will show you. I will make you into a great nation and I will bless you; I will make your name great, and you will be a blessing. I will bless those who bless you, and whoever curses you I will curse; and all peoples on earth will be blessed through you.'"*

From that initial covenant, there follows a predictable pattern of events throughout the Old Testament narrative that includes actions and events that caused the people of God to transgress the terms of the covenant. God speaks to the people, usually through the words of a prophet, warning them to return to the covenant God made with them. The warnings usually come with the threat of some catastrophic event if they don't repent and renew the covenant. Leviticus 26:14-42 provides a rather graphic example of some of those threats.

"If you will not listen to me and carry out all these commands, and if you reject my decrees and abhor my laws and fail to carry out all my commands and so violate my covenant, then I will do this to you: I will bring upon you sudden terror, wasting diseases and fever that will destroy your sight and drain away your life.

I will send a plague among you, and you will be given into enemy hands. I will scatter you among the nations; your land will be laid waste, and your cities will lie in ruins. I will make their hearts so fearful in the lands of their enemies that the sound of a windblown leaf will put them to flight. They will run as though fleeing from the sword, and they will fall, even though no one is pursuing them."

Every litany of threat was followed with a promise of forgiveness and reconciliation. Continuing in Leviticus:

"But if they will confess their sins and the sins of their fathers — their treachery against me and their hostility toward me, which made me hostile toward them so that I sent them into the land of their enemies — then when their uncircumcised hearts are humbled and they pay for their sin, I will remember my covenant with Jacob and my covenant with Isaac and my covenant with Abraham."

There are a number of occasions when the covenant people of God refuse to repent and God follows through with his threat. It is usually an event in nature and it usually has catastrophic results. A classic example is Noah and the flood recorded in Genesis.

As time has progressed, the experiences of the faithful, the traditions of the church, and the developments in the sciences have caused us to revisit our understanding of the sovereign Will of God.

Although, today, we are much better equipped to survive, prepare for, prevent, or even control the events of the natural world, we still have the same inherent desire to know why it happened or what caused it to happen, especially when we find ourselves the victim of what has happened.

So, the questions remains, are catastrophic events the Will of God? Does he cause them? Why doesn't he prevent them? Is it God's Will that bad things happen to good people? Is it God's Will that people suffer? Does God cause every thing that happens, to happen? Why does God heal some people and not others? What is the answer? If we believe God has the ultimate authority to do whatever God wants to do, however God wants to do it, whenever God wants to do it. If we truly believe in the sovereign Will of God, the answer is yes!

Unfortunately, the question of the sovereign Will of God does not end with that simple yes. Rather, it raises two new questions:

1. Does God cause catastrophic things to happen simply because they are the result of the natural order that was set in motion at creation, like a watchmaker who sets a new watch in motion then lays it aside to run on its own, or:
2. Does God cause catastrophic things to happen as the result of a conscious decision on his part because he wants it to happen, when he wants it to happen, how he wants it to happen, in order to get the results that he wants to get? I don't know. But that's okay. For you see, I accept that I am a finite creature, my perception of God is usually distorted, and I am comfortable that the answer to those questions may be one of those things God has chosen to let remain a mystery to me.

Two

Two Other Wills

In chapter one, we explored the Sovereign Will of God: God has the ultimate authority to do whatever God wants to do, however God wants to do it, whenever God wants to do it.

In this chapter, I invite you to join me as we focus our attention on the biblical understanding of two other wills: The predestined Will of God and The free will of humankind.

I would like to begin by taking you on a trip from Springfield, MO, north towards Kansas City, MO, along Highway 13. In particular, a thirty-mile section of the highway between Springfield and Bolivar, MO.

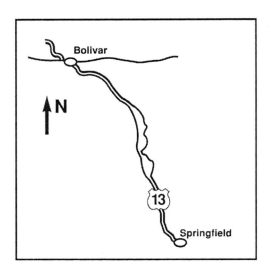

Until a few years ago, except for a few gradual hills and curves, the southbound lane was relatively straight. Conversely, there were two sections of the northbound lane that followed the twists and turns of the old road. There were also a number of side roads and driveways along the way. In some places the two lanes ran side-by-side with a narrow median in between. In other places, especially those where the old road was still being used, the area between the two lanes widened enough that you could not see the other.

Along the straight and narrow section of the southbound lane, the roadway and shoulder are level. Along the old sections of the northbound lanes, some of the shoulders dropped into a ditch or gully. Do you see it? This is an illustration of the predestined Will of God and the free will of humankind.

The Will of God Is...

The southbound lane represents the predestined Will of God. It illustrates what God wants to happen, when He wants it to happen, how He wants it to happen, and what He wants the results to be in our life journey.

Ephesians 1:3-10: *"Praise be to the God and Father of our Lord Jesus Christ, who has blessed us in the heavenly realms with every spiritual blessing in Christ. For he chose us in him before the creation of the world to be holy and blameless in his sight. In love he predestined us to be adopted as his sons through Jesus Christ, in accordance with his pleasure and will, to the praise of his glorious grace, which he has freely given us in the One he loves. In him we have redemption through his blood, the forgiveness of sins, in accordance with the riches of God's grace that he lavished on us with all wisdom and understanding. And he made known to us the mystery of his will according to his good pleasure, which he purposed in Christ, to be put into effect when the times will have reached their fulfillment-to bring all things in heaven and on earth together under one head, even Christ."*.

I want you to note two key passages and how they relate to the predestined Will of God:

1. Verse 5: In love he *predestined* us to be adopted as his sons through Jesus Christ, in accordance with his *pleasure*

2. Verse 9: And he made known to us the mystery of his *will* according to His Good *pleasure*.

The Greek word for pleasure in the context of this passage is *eudokia* (yoo-dok-ee'-ah) which means desire. The desire of God as understood to be the predestined Will of God.

Let's take just a minute to explore the word *predestined*. I do not see scriptural evidence that the predestined Will of God means that God randomly chooses who will receive eternal life and who will not. I do understand the confusion many have regarding the concept of predestination, a confusion that centers on the biblical term "foreknowledge." A classic example is the salutation to 1 Peter 1:1-2: *"Peter, an apostle of Jesus Christ, To God's elect, strangers in the world... who have been chosen according to the foreknowledge of God the Father, through the sanctifying work of the Spirit, for obedience to Jesus Christ and sprinkling by his blood:"*

The biblical understanding of foreknowledge is that because God is a sovereign God, he has the ability to know all events, including the free acts of man, before they happen. Let me repeat that! The biblical understanding of foreknowledge is that because God is a sovereign God, he has the ability to know all events, including the free will acts of man, before they happen. It does not necessarily mean that God has decided ahead of time what we

The Will of God Is...

will do, when we will do it, how we will do it, or what the results will be, regardless of any decision we may make along the way.

In reality, it appears to me that the scripture teaches the predestined Will of God is a one-size-fits-all, desire of God. We will examine that in more detail beginning with chapter four.

The southbound lane of Highway 13 represents the predestined Will of God. The northbound lane of Highway 13 represents the free will of humankind.

You may find it interesting to note that in the nine translations I reviewed, the term free will does not appear anywhere in scripture. The concept of free will finds it origins in the Garden of Eden. Genesis 2:15-17: *"The LORD God took the man and put him in the Garden of Eden to work it and take care of it. And the LORD God commanded the man, 'You are free to eat from any tree in the garden; but you must not eat from the tree of the knowledge of good and evil, for when you eat of it you will surely die.'"*

You know the story. Adam did eat of the forbidden tree and Genesis 3:22 tells us what the consequences were: *"And the Lord God said, 'The man has now become like one of us, knowing good and evil'"*.

The concept of the free will of humankind has evolved into the doctrine of the free will of humankind, because the assumption is made that if humankind has knowledge of good and evil, humankind has the free will to choose between good and evil. This assumption is affirmed in scripture by the use of the word "if."

Deuteronomy 30:9-10: *"Then the Lord your God will make you most prosperous in all the work of your hands and in the fruit of your womb, the young of your livestock and the crops of your land. The Lord will again delight in you and make you prosperous, just as he delighted in your fathers, **if** you obey the Lord your God and keep his commands and decrees that are written in this Book of the Law and turn to the Lord your God with all your heart and with all your soul."*

John 15:5-8: *"I am the vine; you are the branches. **If** a man remains in me and me in him, he will bear much fruit; apart from me you can do nothing. **If** anyone does not remain in me, he is like a branch that is thrown away and withers; such branches are picked up, thrown into the fire and burned. **If** you remain in me and my words remain in you, ask whatever you wish, and it will be given you."*

Romans 10:9-11: *"**If** you confess with your mouth, 'Jesus is Lord,' and believe in your heart that God raised him from the dead, you will be saved. For it is with your heart that you believe and are justified, and it is with your mouth that you confess and are saved."*

Matthew 16:24-25: Then Jesus said to his disciples, *"**If** anyone would come after me, he must deny himself and take up his cross and follow me."*

In each example and many more, the use of the word **if** in the context of the scripture implies choice or free will. The northbound lane of Highway 13 represents the free will of humankind.

In the middle or median, the area that separates the two lanes of traffic, is sin. According to scripture, sin is the transgression of God's will, either by omitting to do what God's law requires, or by doing what it forbids: The theological concepts of omission or commission.

In Isaiah 59:1-2, the prophet declares: *"Surely the arm of the LORD is not too short to save, nor his ear too dull to hear. But your iniquities* (the Old Testament word for sin) *have **separated** you from your God;"*

What that says to me is that sin is in the middle of the predestined Will of God and the free will of humankind, constantly pushing against the free will of mankind, trying to destroy or distort the righteousness of God. The righteousness of God is God's desire that humankind be in a right or connected relationship with God, which is the goal of the predestined Will of God.

It also may explain a term we have all heard many times. If sin creates enough of a separation between the predestined Will of God and the free will of humankind, humankind will begin to slide down the shoulder until the other lane is completely out of site: Apparently when that happens, humankind slides backwards: thus the term "backsliding."

One final point: After my decision to use Highway 13 as an illustration, I discovered that in the tradition of Judaism, the number 13 is the number for love, which raises some interesting possibilities:

1. The relationship between God and humankind is rooted in love.
2. The classic passage of scripture about love, what some call the love chapter - is 1 Corinthians 13.
3. If the number 13 is associated with the love of God, is that why the pagan world created a superstition that the number 13 should be avoided?

I don't know, but that's okay. For you see, I accept that I am a finite creature and I am comfortable that answers to some of my questions may be one of those things that God has chosen to let remain a mystery to u

Three

The Grace Package

As we travel along the road of our life journey, there are two important mile makers along the way. The first is the point in our life journey when we recognize that there is a right way and a wrong way, we realize that we have the ability to choose between the two, and we understand that there are consequences to our choices. Some faith communities refer to this point in our life journey as the age of accountability. If we recognize, realize, and understand the concept of right and wrong, we are accountable for our decisions.

The second important mile marker is when we are offered a road hazard package called grace, a package that is offered to us free of charge, with no pre-approval required, and no restrictions because of pre-existing conditions. As a matter of fact, it is the pre-existing condition of our life that qualifies us for the package. It is free of charge because it has been prepaid by God in Christ.

Colossians 1:14: *"God has purchased our freedom with his blood and has forgiven all our sins."* Ephesians 2:8-10: *"God saved you by his special favor when you believed. And you can't take credit for this; it is a gift from God. Salvation is not a reward for the good things we have done, so none of us can boast about it. For we are God's masterpiece. He has created us anew in Christ Jesus, so that we can do the good things he planned for us long ago."*

This grace package includes four benefits:

1. If we accept it, our past driving record will be expunged.
Psalm 32:1-2: *"Oh, what joy for those whose rebellion is forgiven, whose sin is put out of sight! Yes, what joy for those whose record the LORD has cleared of sin…"*
Romans 3:23-25: *"For all have sinned; all fall short of God's glorious standard. Yet now God in his gracious kindness declares us not guilty. He has done this through Christ Jesus, who has freed us by taking away our sins."* It's as though we are on a totally new page, the old one forgotten, gone, and destroyed!
2 Corinthians 5:17-18: *"Therefore, if anyone is in Christ, he is a new creation; the old has gone, the new has come! All this is from God, who reconciled us to himself*

The Will of God Is...

through Christ and gave us the ministry of reconciliation."

2. If we accept the grace package, we will be provided with a comprehensive owner's manual. A divine owner's manual that contains instructions, procedures, guidelines, and checklist for all models. A divine owner's manual that is written in a language that all groups of people can read and understand the same directions. A divine owner's manual that contains a section on PM (Preventative Maintenance), troubleshooting complete with a checklist that if followed can fix what is broken. A divine owner's manual that includes a detailed map, complete with warnings of sharp curves, pot holes, detours, side roads, and dangerous intersections. A divine owner's manual that contains hundreds of testimonials of those who have traveled the road before. A divine owner's manual that includes the predestined Will of God and 66 chapters of instruction on how to make *"thy will be done on earth, as it is in heaven."* The manual is the Bible!

3. If we accept the grace package, we will be connected to a divine GPS. We will have at our disposal, 24/7, access to God's Personal Spirit, the Holy Spirit. A GPS that will empower us on our journey: Acts 1:8: *"... when the Holy Spirit has come upon you, you*

will receive power." A GPS that will guide us on our journey: John 14:23-26: *"All those who love me will do what I say* (predestined Will of God). *My Father will love them, and we come to them and live with them. This message is from the Father who sent me. I am telling you these things now while I am still with you. But when the Father sends the Counselor as my representative — and by the Counselor I mean the Holy Spirit — he will teach you everything and will remind you of everything I myself have told you."*

A GPS that comes with a life-time guarantee. Ephesians 1:13b-14: *"...when you believed in Christ, he identified you as his own by giving you the Holy Spirit, whom he promised long ago. The Spirit is God's guarantee that he will give us everything he promised and that he has purchased us to be his own people."* (NLT)

4. If we accept the grace package, we will never have to travel our journey alone. We will become part of a convoy of faith. The generic definition of convoy is a group organized for protection in moving. When we accept the grace package, we become part of a group who is traveling on the same life road as we are: A group who is relying on the same road hazard grace package that is offered to us. A wonderful community of

faith who will give us a jump start when our battery is low, a community of faith who will give us a ride when we are broke down, a community of faith who will be our guard rail when we begin to veer of the road, and a wrecker to pull us out of the ditch when we have slid off the road. Acts 2:44-47: *"And all the believers lived in a wonderful harmony, holding everything in common. They sold whatever they owned and pooled their resources so that each person's need was met. They followed a daily discipline of worship in the Temple followed by meals at home, every meal a celebration, exuberant and joyful, as they praised God. People in general liked what they saw. Every day their number grew as God added those who were saved."* (MSG)

Is that awesome or what? An amazing divine road hazard package called grace. Amazing grace! You know what is even more amazing to me? The fact that many people choose to reject it. Even when it is offered over and over again, they still choose to reject it. I just don't understand, but I suppose that is okay because there are a lot of things about the Will of God I don't understand.

What I have found on my Will of God journey is that virtually every biblical reference to the Will of God points to the same thing. The predestined Will of God is contained within the *Decalogue*, from the Greek word which means "Ten Words," recorded in Exodus 20:1-17. Yes! You read right! I am talking about the Ten Commandments.

Although God gave the Ten Commandments to His people through Moses at Mount Sinai more than 3,000 years ago, they are still relevant today. They have an abiding significance, for God's character is unchangeable. These laws originate from God and from His eternal character; therefore, their moral value cannot change.

About 1,300 years after God gave the laws, Jesus affirmed them. Matthew 5:17-18: *"Do not think that I have come to abolish the Law or the Prophets; I have not come to abolish them but to fulfill them."*

The predestined Will of God - The free will of humankind. With all that said and done, the question still remains: What does God want us to do? What is the Will of God? Here's my take on it.

Four

The Will of God is... No other gods!

What does God want to happen, when He wants it to happen, how He wants it to happen, and what does He want the results to be in our relationship with others?

Let's begin by looking at a little Jewish History. The occasion of the giving of the Decalogue or ten words occurred after the nation of Israel was released from Egyptian slavery and had been wandering in the wilderness of the Sinai Peninsula for about 5-10 years.

The Israelites had been in Egypt for over 200 years. In many ways, they were more Egyptian than they were Jew. Other than the oral traditions handed down from one generation to another, the only way of life any of them knew was Egyptian.

Although they were in slavery, they had never known anything else. As a matter of fact, there is strong historical evidence that when Moses confronted the people with God's plan to leave, many of them protested and refused to go. On the other hand, we are told in Exodus 12 that many of the Egyptians were so glad to see them go, they gave the departing Israelites gifts of gold, silver, and clothing.

One confusing tradition in Egyptian culture was the practice of Polytheism and Henotheism: Big words that have simple meanings. Polytheism means the belief in and worship of more than one God. Henotheism means the belief in more than one god but the worship of only one. By one count there were over twenty-three separate gods worshiped in Egyptian culture.

When the Monotheistic or one god traditions of the Jewish God Yahweh were taught, many of the Israelites understood them to mean that there was more than one god, and the one they were to worship was Yahweh. Thus the practice of Henotheism was common among the Egyptian Jews.

Consequently, the predestined Will of God was, and is, first and foremost, "You shall have no other gods before me." The Hebrew word for before can also mean besides. What that means is that you shall not acknowledge the existence of, or express belief in, any other divine being as being more sovereign than me, or as being equal to me. You shall have no other gods before or besides me. The God of Israel is the one and only sovereign God of authority in the world.

It is interesting to note that the ten plagues that preceded the release of the Israelites had a double purpose: One was to convince the Egyptians to let

The Will of God Is...

the Israelites go. Two, each of the plagues involved an Egyptian god in some manner, showing how powerless they were in comparison to Israel's God. Exodus 18:11-12: Jethro, Moses' father-in-law is speaking: *"Now I know that the Lord is greater than all other gods, for he did this to those who had treated Israel arrogantly."*

Knowing the inclination of humankind, God took the "no other gods" directive a step further. In addition to not acknowledging the existence of, or expressing belief in, any other divine being before or besides him, God commanded that nothing, whether present in the natural world or created by humankind, should ever become an artificial or counterfeit god. Exodus 20:4-5a: *"You shall not make for yourself an idol in the form of anything in heaven above or on the earth beneath or in the waters below. You shall not bow down to them or worship them."*

In the years preceding the Exodus, Egypt was under constant attack from a group known only as the "Sea People." With their repeated invasions, insecurity grew and Egyptian culture began to change. In particular, the desire of immortality became less associated with religion and more with magic rituals. People began to believe they could pass into paradise with the right charms in their coffins instead of leading a good life.

Consequently, they began to reason, if these manmade charms could guarantee immortality, maybe they could also protect them while they were still alive. That in turn evolved into animism, the attribution of conscious life to inanimate objects in nature. Walt Disney built an entertainment empire with making inanimate objects come alive. He called it animation.

The Egyptians began to believe that if inanimate objects in nature had conscious life in them, then charms or graven (carved) images made from objects in nature could also have conscious life within them. From that there evolved the practice of divination, the attribution of divine qualities and powers to inanimate objects.

Thus, the stage is set for God to command, Exodus 20:4-5:"*You shall not make for yourself a carved image — any likeness of anything that is in heaven above, or that is in the earth beneath, or that is in the water under the earth; you shall not bow down to them nor serve them.*" (NKJV)

"You shall have no other gods before me." Shall is a contemporary legal term that originated in Jewish law, and means no exception, no options, no mitigating circumstances. You either do it or you don't.

Exodus 20: 5b-6: "*I, the LORD your God, am a jealous God, punishing the children for the sin of the fathers to the third and fourth generation of those who hate me and do not keep my commandments. For those who do, I will show my love to a thousand generations of those who love me and keep my commandments.*"

The Will of God Is...

Do you see it? What is the Will of God? No other gods. How can we show God that we love him? Keep His commandments - do His Will!

I have always found the "thousand generations" statement in vs. 6 to be intriguing, so I did a little research on it. According to calculations based on Matthew 1:17, a Biblical generation is 51.4 years. Since scholars date the Exodus somewhere around 1300 BC, when you add 1300 + 2013, and divide by 51.4, it turns out that there have been 65 generations since God promised to show his love to a thousand generations of those who love him and keep his commandments.

Consequently, there are 48,059 years of God's love left for those who keep his commandments. It would seem to me that if nothing else, that confirms that what God said he wants to happen, when He wants it to happen, how He wants it to happen, and what He wants the results to be in our relationship with him and with others is still in effect, is still relevant, and is the eternal, unchanging, predestined Will of God!

The Will of God is... No other gods!

Five

The Will of God is... Don't Abuse My Name!

What is the predestined Will of God?

Exodus 20:7: *"Thou shalt not take the name of the Lord thy God in vain; for the Lord will not hold him guiltless that taketh his name in vain."* (KJV)

Exodus 20:7: *"You shall not make wrongful use of the name of the Lord your God, for the Lord will not acquit anyone who misuses his name."* (NRSV)

Exodus 20:7: *"You shall not misuse the name of the LORD your God, for the LORD will not hold anyone guiltless who misuses his name."* (NIV)

Exodus 20:7: *"Do not misuse the name of the LORD your God. The LORD will not let you go unpunished if you misuse his name."* (NLT)

Doesn't matter how you say it, the Will of God is... Don't abuse my name! Exodus 20:5b is a perplexing statement: *"I, the LORD your God, am a jealous God."* Does the thought of God being a jealous God bother you? What does God have to be jealous of?

The Will of God Is...

Jealously is included in the seven woes taught by Jesus in Matthew's gospel (Matthew 23:13-32). In 1 Corinthians 13:6, jealously is identified as one of the examples of what love is not. In Galatians chapter 5:22, jealously is listed as one of the examples of a sinful nature. Jealously is a violation of the 10th commandment! (Exodus 20:17) So, what's up with this jealous God thing? Here's my take on it.

In the original Hebrew there are two words that can be translated into our English word *jealousy*. Both are pronounced the same: kawnaw *(kaw-naw)*. One is spelled qa-na, the other is qa-nna.

Qana means jealous <u>of</u>, and relates to interpersonal relationships. That's the one we are the most familiar with: A negative quality characterized by unhealthy suspicion, envy, being overprotective, and generally making life miserable for everyone who might be unfortunate enough to be the target of ones jealously.

Qanna means jealous <u>for</u>. In the context of our Exodus passage it applies to the nature of God and His relationship with his people. Qanna is sometimes translated into the Greek as zelos *(ze-los)*, which is the origin of the word zealous, which means an out-and-out, unreserved, unrestricted commitment to a person, group, or cause.

When the scripture says God is a jealous God, it means he is out-and-out, unreserved, unrestricted, committed to something. The prophet Zechariah tells us that God is zealous for his people! He is zealous in his protection of them and zealous in his compassion for them.

Zechariah 1:14: *"Then the angel who was speaking to me said, "Proclaim this word: This is what the LORD Almighty says: 'I am very jealous for Jerusalem and Zion..."*

Zechariah 8:1-2: *"Again, the word of the LORD Almighty came to me. This is what the LORD Almighty says: "I am very jealous for Zion; I am burning with jealousy for her."* In both the Zechariah passages, the word Zion means the eternal kingdom of God; the eternal family of God.

When we move into the letters of Paul we find that he apparently understood the concept of God as a jealous God, and wanted to emulate it in his relationship with the Corinthian churches. 2 Corinthians 11:2: *"I am jealous for you with a godly jealousy."*

As I have reflected on this idea of a godly jealousy; being zealous in protection and zealous in compassion, I have found myself asking the question, besides my family, friends, and church family, what is it that I am most jealous for? The answer I came up with is my name. I am jealous for my name. I think we are all that way when it comes to our name, because our name is the icon of our identity.

Ecclesiastes 7:1: *"A good name is better than precious ointment or fine perfume."*

In Old Testament thought, a name means existence. Nothing exists without a name. In the

Genesis accounts of creation (Genesis 1:1-25), none of the creative process was complete until it was given a name. *And God said, "Let there be light," and there was light. God named the light "<u>day</u>," and the darkness he named "<u>night</u>." And God said, "Let the water under the sky be gathered to one place, and let dry ground appear." And it was so. God named the dry ground "<u>land</u>," and the gathered waters he named "<u>seas</u>."*

Then God said, "Let the land produce vegetation: seed-bearing plants and trees on the land that bear fruit with seed in it, according to their various kinds." And God created the great creatures of the sea and every living and moving thing with which the water teems, according to their kinds, and God said, let the land produce living creatures according to their kinds: livestock, creatures that move along the ground, and wild animals, each according to its kind." In those last three passages, the phrase "according to their kinds" means according to their specific names. I think scientists refer to "their kinds" as species, genus, and phylum. Our name is the icon of our identity because it reflects our very existence.

When my wife retired, we both had to get new certified copies of our birth certificates. When I went to the local health department to get them, they informed me that I did not legally exist because my name was not in the state database of births. I laughed! They didn't think it was funny. I had to write a letter to the state proving that I existed because according to them, I didn't have a name.

Our name is the icon of our identity because it is a reflection of our character and personality. I recently found a baby name web site that lists 5,200 male and female names, each with a list of particular personality traits and characteristics associated with each name.

There are a number of instances in scripture where after an encounter with God a persons name is changed to reflect a change in their personality and character. Abram became Abraham. Sari became Sarah, Simon became Peter. Saul became Paul.

Our name is also the icon of our identity in terms of authority. To speak or act in someone's name is to act as a representative of that person and thus assume a part of their authority.

God spoke these words: I, the Lord your God, am a jealous God. You shall not misuse the name of the Lord your God. Don't abuse my name. Do you see it? Just as our name is the icon of our identity because it reflects our very existence, so it is with God. Over and over again in scripture, the name of God is used as a synonym for his presence. Just as our name is the icon of our identity because it is a reflection of our character and personality, so it is with God. We call that character and personality of God the revealed nature of God.

Just as the name of someone we are associated with is a reflection of who we are, so it is with our relationship with God. As disciples of Jesus Christ, who we are is a reflection of who God is.

To profane means to pollute. Isn't it sad that sometimes the ones who profane the name of God and pollute the system the worst, are those who are supposed to be associated with him the most? You think that is why Paul admonished the Colossian Christians (Colossians 3:16-17) to, *"let the word of Christ dwell in you richly ... And whatever you do, whether in word or deed, do it all in the name of the Lord Jesus..."*

Just as our name is also the icon of our identity in terms of authority, so it is with God. He has given us the keys of the kingdom and all the rights and privileges that go with them. In doing so, he has empowered us to act as his representatives with his authority as stewards of his kingdom. Matthew 16:19: *"I will give you the keys of the kingdom of heaven; whatever you bind on earth will be bound in heaven, and whatever you loose on earth will be loosed in heaven."* I, the Lord your God, am a jealous God. You shall not misuse the name of the Lord your God.

Beginning to see the picture? To misuse the name of God encompasses much more than simply giving God the last name of damn! God has revealed himself to us through his word, tradition, and experience. He has revealed himself to us through the person of Jesus. He reveals himself to us through the presence and power of the Holy Spirit.

When we pray, and finish our prayer by saying some variation of, in Jesus name, we are approaching the throne of God with our petitions and intercessions under the authority granted us by Jesus.

When we say, I swear to tell the truth, so help me God, we are using the authority of God as verification of our truthfulness. When someone sneezes and we say, God, bless you, we are calling on the authority of God to bless them.

If we pray with wrong motives, if our Yes does not mean Yes and our No does not mean No; if we misuse or abuse the authority of God, we are guilty of causing the power and glory of his name to be brought into question, because we have compromised and marginalized the integrity of the Will of God!

How do we avoid abusing God's name? By being jealous! Jealous of his name with a godly jealousy. Zealous in protecting the integrity of God's name in our words and deeds. Zealous in our compassion for others in our words and deeds.

What is the Will of God? Don't Abuse my Name!

Six

The Will of God is... Go to Church!

Many years ago, on the last day of a summer school class, the instructor ask a predictable question: "What did you come here looking for, and did you find it?" Needless to say, there were as many different answers as there were persons answering the question. The one answer that intrigued me the most was a lady who said, "I came here to find Sabbath, and I did." "I came here to find Sabbath, and I did."

After class, I caught up with her at lunch and asked her what she meant. She told me that for her, Sabbath meant the opportunity to gather with a community of believers, in a special place, with a single focus of mind and spirit, and experience the presence of God in a way she could not experience in any other way, at any other time, in any other place.

I then asked her, don't you think you can worship God and experience his presence anywhere, at any time? Yes, she said. Absolutely: You can worship

God and experience his presence anywhere, at any time. But you cannot have a Sabbath anywhere, at any time. What is the Will of God? Go to church.

Let's begin with a brief review of the fourth commandment, from which we are taking our Will of God answer for this chapter. The fourth commandment is unique among the other ten because it is the only one that decrees the observance of a specific day, set aside for a specific purpose. We call it Sabbath; in Hebrew it is pronounced Shabbat (*Shabbat*). In the *Mitzvah*, the Hebrew term for all 613 of the commandments, there are detailed instructions for the observance of fourteen different festivals and holy days. Shabbat is the most important ritual observance in Judaism because it is the only one instituted in the Ten Commandments.

The Shabbat commandment has been interpreted and reinterpreted more than any of the other 613 Mitzvah. Think about it! It required interpretation the moment it was given. What does Sabbath or Shabbat mean? Which six day period are we talking about? What day of the week do we begin counting? How long is it supposed to last? Does it include pot luck? How are we supposed to do it?

The Shabbat commandment is unique among the other ten because it is one of the few that when listed in the Deuteronomy version, it has a different rationale than the Exodus version. Exodus 20:8-11: *"Remember the Sabbath day by keeping it holy. For in six days the LORD made the heavens and the earth, the sea, and all that is in them, but he rested on the seventh day. Therefore the LORD blessed the Sabbath day and made it holy."* Deuteronomy 5:12-15: *"Observe the Sabbath day by keeping it holy. Remember that you were slaves in Egypt and that the LORD your God brought you out of there with a mighty hand and an outstretched arm. Therefore the LORD your God has commanded you to observe the Sabbath day."* Let's do a little interpretation of our own:

1) What does Sabbath or Shabbat mean? When we incorporate our definition of worship into my friend's description, Shabbat becomes: the opportunity to gather with a community of believers, in a special place, with a single focus of mind and spirit, and experience the presence of God and respond to the presence of God in a way we cannot experience in any other way, at any other time, in any other place.
2) Which six day period are we talking about? What day of the week do we begin counting? Personally, I don't think it matters! I have trouble believing there is anything sacred about which day of the week a community of believers gathers to have Sabbath. Hebrews 10:23-25: *"Therefore, brothers, Let us hold unswervingly to the hope we profess, for he who promised is faithful.*

> *And let us consider how we may spur one another on toward love and good deeds. Let us not give up meeting together, as some are in the habit of doing, but let us encourage one another-and all the more as you see the Day approaching."*
>
> What does concern me more than the specific day we observe Sabbath, is the individuals and groups who have allowed the specific day of Sabbath to become a divisive issue within the Christian community.
>
> 3) How long is it supposed to last? Contrary to popular belief, there is not a Mitzvah that says, Remember the Sabbath day by keeping it holy, and do it in an hour or less! Here is a description of a typical contemporary Jewish Sabbath.

At about 2 or 3 pm on Friday afternoon, Shabbat preparations begin. The mood is much like preparing for the arrival of a special guest: the house is cleaned, the family bathes and dresses up, the best dishes and tableware are set out, and a festive meal is prepared. In addition, everything that cannot be done during Shabbat is done in advance. Shabbat, like all Jewish days, begins at sunset, because in the story of creation in Genesis chapter 1, it says, *"And there was evening, and there was morning, one day."* From this, the inference is made that a day begins with evening, that is, sunset.

The Will of God Is...

About 18-20 minutes before sunset, a blessing is recited and the women of the house light two candles, representing the two different versions in Exodus and Deuteronomy. Once that is completed, Shabbat officially begins. The family then attends an evening service at the synagogue, which can last anywhere from one to two hours.

After services, the family comes home for dinner. Before dinner, the man of the house sanctifies the Shabbat by reciting a prayer over wine and two loaves of Challot *(chal-lay)* bread. The family then eats a dinner of stewed or slow cooked items, because of the prohibition against cooking during Shabbat.

After dinner, a Shabbat blessing is recited. By the time all of this is completed, it may be 9 pm or later. The family has an hour or two to talk or study scripture, and then go to sleep. The next morning Shabbat services at the synagogue begin around 9 am and continue until about noon. Did you catch that: From nine o'clock to noon – three hours! After services, the community has pot luck. By the time the meal is finished, it is about 2 pm.

The family then returns home and studies the scripture for a while, talks, takes an afternoon walk, plays games, or takes an afternoon nap. You know why Sabbath afternoon naps are so good? Because it is the day God created to rest!

Shabbat ends at nightfall, when three stars are visible, approximately 40 minutes after sunset. So

Shabbat is approximately 24 hours long, four to five of which are spent at church!

Let's review:

- ✓ What does Sabbath or Shabbat mean?
- ✓ Which six day period are we talking about?
- ✓ What day of the week do we begin counting?
- ✓ How long is it supposed to last?
- ✓ Does in include pot luck?

The only thing left on my checklist is: How are we supposed to do it? It is here that we reconcile the two versions of the Shabbat commandment. In the Exodus passage, we are called to Sabbath to zakhor *(zak-hor)* or remember. In the Deuteronomy passage, we are called to Sabbath to shamor *(sha-mor)* or observe.

As I have tried to understand it, to remember and observe translates into a predestined Will of God that calls us to take a deliberate and intentional break from the routine of our daily life in order to gather with a community of believers, in a special place, with a single focus of mind and spirit, and experience the presence of God and respond to the presence of God in a way we cannot experience in any other way, at any other time, in any other place.

Apparently it was important that the people were deliberate and intentional not only in how they celebrated Shabbat, but also in the ways they took a break from the routine of their daily lives. In the

The Will of God Is...

Talmud, the collection of rabbinical interpretations of the law, there are thirty-nine categories of acts forbidden on the Sabbath.

I would like to propose that remember and observe might also mean to gather as a community of believers in order to think about, recollect, focus on, and remind each other that we are to love the Lord our God with all our heart and with all our soul and with all our mind and with all our strength. To think about, recollect, focus on, and remind each other that we are to love others as we love ourselves. To think about, recollect, focus on, and remind each other that just as God was the agent of creation in the beginning, so he is the agent of renewal, restoration, and empowerment in the present *(the rationale in the Exodus version).*

To think about, recollect, focus on, and remind each other of the gift of grace that God has consistently given his people through-out the ages; whether it be grace in the form of freedom from slavery in Egypt *(the rationale in the Deuteronomy version)* or whether it be the freedom that forgiveness gives, the freedom that redemption offers, and the assurance of eternal freedom through God's gift of grace in the person of Jesus.

Sabbath gives us the opportunity to remember and observe that regardless of what valley we may find our life journey taking us through, we will never have to walk alone. Sabbath is gathering together with a community of believers!

One final question: Is it necessary that we have Sabbath every week? Is it really that important that we remember and observe in a deliberate and intentional way every seven days? Do we need to be in church every week? Yes! Why? Because sometimes, the only way we can make it through the other six days, is to spend part of the seventh gathered with our local community of believers.

Do we need to have Sabbath every week? Do we need to be in church every week? Yes! Why? Because it is the Will of God!

Seven

The Will of God is... Family!

In 1996, Hillary Clinton published a book entitled, *It Takes a Village and Other Lessons Children Teach Us*. The title and main theme of the book were taken from an old African proverb that states, "It takes a whole village to raise a child." In her book, Clinton writes: "I chose that old African proverb to title my book because it offers a timeless reminder that children will thrive only if their families thrive and if the whole of society cares enough to provide for them. The sage who first offered that proverb would undoubtedly be bewildered by what constitutes the modern village. In earlier times and places, and until recently in our own culture, the "village" meant an actual geographic place where individuals and families lived and worked together.

"For most of us, though, the village doesn't look like that anymore. In fact, it's difficult to paint a picture of the modern village; so frantic and fragmented has much of our culture become. Extended families rarely live in the same town, let alone the same house. In many communities, crime and fear keep us behind locked doors. Where we used to chat with neighbors on stoops and porches, now we watch videos in our darkened living rooms. Instead of strolling down Main Street, we spend hours in automobiles and at anonymous shopping malls. We don't join civic associations, churches, unions, political parties, or even bowling leagues the way we used to.

"To many, this brave new world seems dehumanizing and inhospitable. It is not surprising, then, that there is a yearning for the 'good old days' as a refuge from the problems of the present. But by turning away, we blind ourselves to the continuing, evolving presence of the village in our lives, and its critical importance for how we live together.

"The village can no longer be defined as a place on a map, or as a list of people or organizations, but its essence remains the same: it is the network of values and relationships that support and affect our lives."[2]

The Lord said to Moses, "Speak to the entire assembly of Israel and say to them: Honor your father and your mother, so that you may live long in the land the Lord your God is giving you. What is the predestined Will of God? It is family!

I would like to make four proposals to you regarding the family component of the Will of God:

First, I would like to propose that before it was the title of a book, even before it was an African proverb, "It takes a whole village to raise a child" could have been a description of how the early community of faith understood their relationship with God and with each other.

Second, I would like to propose that it is more than mere coincidence that the commandment to honor your father and your mother is positioned between the first four and the last five. The birth of a child was viewed by the early community of faith as a partnership with God.

The material substance was derived from the parents, and it was God who provided the soul and spirit. We see this partnership reflected in the account of the creation of humankind. Genesis 2:7: *"The Lord God formed the man from the dust of the ground;* (material substance). *God breathed into his nostrils the breath of life;* (soul and spirit); *and the man became a living being."*

For many years, the common and accepted understanding of when life begins was called quickening. Quickening was the point in the development of a human being when the mother first experienced movement in her womb. It was believed that quickening occurred when God breathed into the nostrils of the child the breath of life and granted them their soul and spirit. Their spirit was the empowerment to transform their material DNA into a unique individual. Their soul was their spiritual DNA, their unique inner point of contact through which they would experience their relationship with God.

You see the connection? You see how the birth of a child could be viewed by the early community of faith as a partnership with God? Consequently, the partnership commandment to honor your father and your mother became a tool in understanding humankind's relationship with God, and an affirmation that we are created to be part of a connected community called family.

Proposal number three: The belief in the partnership of God and man in the birth of a child gives us insight into the Biblical understanding that the responsibility for the raising of a child was a community partnership. When the fifth commandment says honor your father and your mother, the meaning and understanding of father and mother was much more all inclusive than it is today. For the early community of faith, a child's biological father and mother were viewed as a single unit that was part of a larger community of parental responsibility.

While Judaism was a patriarchal society in which men were granted complete authority in affairs of government and religion, when it came to the family, father and mother were viewed as a single unit with equal authority. In Exodus 20:12, father and mother are listed together. The Hebrew word for "and" in this context is a legal term implying joint ownership. When the command is repeated in Leviticus 19:3, mother is listed first, implying an interchangeable partnership of equal authority. *"Each of you must respect his mother and father…"*

As we move into the New Testament, Paul explains the Old Testament partnership of father and mother or mother and father, as a single unit called parents. Ephesians 6:1: *"Children, obey your parents in the Lord, for this is right."* Why is it right? Because it is the Will of God, which Paul affirms in the following verse when he quotes Exodus 20:12. Ephesians 6:2-3: *"Honor your father and mother "-which is the first commandment with a promise- that it may go well with you and that you may enjoy long life on the earth."*

Beginning to see the family photo emerge? It's beginning to look like one of those family reunion photos. Do you see it? Surrounding mom, dad, and the kids is their extended family, the village, their community of faith.

Our community connection is reinforced in the passage from Leviticus 19, when honor your mother and father is linked to observing the Sabbath in a connectional partnership: *"Each of you must respect his mother and father, and you must observe my Sabbaths."*

What is Sabbath? The opportunity to gather with a community of believers, in a special place, with a single focus of mind and spirit, and experience the presence of God and respond to the presence of God in a way we cannot experience in any other way, at any other time, in any other place. You see it? The opportunity to gather with a community of believers.

In her book, Mrs. Clinton makes the statement, "parents, first and foremost, are responsible for their children. But we are all responsible for ensuring that children are raised in a nation that doesn't just talk about family values, but acts in ways that values families."[2]

When a Jewish baby boy was circumcised within the first week of his life, it marked them as a member of the community of God's people. When a young child is presented for dedication now days, their parents are asked two important questions:

1. "Do you therefore accept as your duty and privilege to live before him or her a life that becomes the Gospel; to exercise all godly care that he or she be brought up in the Christian faith, that he or she be taught the holy scriptures, and that he or she learn to give reverent attendance upon the private and public worship of God?"
2. "Will you endeavor to keep this child under the ministry and guidance of the Church until he or she by the power of God shall accept for himself or herself the gift of salvation, and be confirmed as a full and responsible member of Christ's holy church?"

The Will of God Is...

Two questions that demand life-long commitments that are critical to the spiritual health and well being of that child. The very same life-long commitment that is ask of the child's community of faith!

One final proposal: In the context of the Will of God, when does a child cease to be a child and when does our responsibility end, as a community of faith, to nurture them and live before them a life that becomes the Gospel? I believe the scripture has a clear answer: When that child takes their last breath on earth, regardless of their age! The King James Version of Leviticus 19:1 says: *"Speak unto all the congregation of the <u>children</u> of Israel."*

In Matthew 25:35-36, Jesus says, when they are hungry, give them something to eat, when they are thirsty give them something to drink, when they are a stranger invite them in, when they need clothes, clothe them, when they are sick, look after them, when they are in the prison of fear, pain, discouragement, guilt, and hopelessness, be there for them.

You suppose Moses and Jesus might be proposing that it really does take a whole village to raise a child, from birth to death, regardless of their age?

The Will of God is Family!

Eight

The Will of God is...
Be a Lover, not a Fighter!

Hanging on the wall in my office is a piece of wood painted red. It's a recycled yard-stick. I call it a "what-if stick!" Have you ever used one? A few years ago, I was visiting with a friend who was using a "what-if" stick to beat up on herself.

You know what I am talking about? What if I had done it another way? *Bam!* What if I hadn't done it that way? *Wop!* What if I had made a different decision? *Smack!* What if I had waited a little longer? *Pow!* What if – What if, What if: You know what I am talking about? You ever beat up on yourself with the "what-if" stick?

It's not a pretty sight. When the beating is over, most folks end up knocking all the success and joy out of their life to the point that the only thing that is left is an ugly pile of failure and unhappiness. Most of us will beat up on ourselves for a while, nurse our wounds, and then go on with life. The person I was visiting with had been

The Will of God Is...

beating up on herself with the "what-if" stick for over forty years.

When I said nobody is that bad, her response was, "I bet you have never broken all ten of the commandments!" "Oh yes I have," I replied: "All ten of them?" "All ten of them! I bet you have never killed someone!"

A survey was conducted a few years ago in which the respondents were asked to rank the Ten Commandments, from first to last, that they had not broken or would be least likely to break. Over 95% listed: You shall not kill as number one on their list. I have a feeling if we could take that same survey here, the results would be the same.

I have thought about that, and I have come to a conclusion! The 95% who listed: You shall not kill as the commandment they would be least likely to break, were dreadfully wrong. I would like to suggest to you that from the perspective of Jesus, the number one commandment humankind has broken the most and the one humankind will be most likely to break again, is: You shall not kill, and the weapon of choice is words!

"Sticks and stones may break my bones but words will never hurt me." Ever heard that one? Ever really believed it? Until I researched its origin, I was convinced that it was written by a hermit who lived all his life in a cave, void of any contact with another human being. That had to be the only way they could honestly say that words never hurt. Words can hurt. Words do hurt!

"Sticks and stones may break my bones but words will never hurt me," is believed to be an old African proverb that was brought to America by the slaves. It was taught to young black children in the south as a means for coping with words: Hurtful, demeaning, racial words that the young blacks would hear from their bigoted white neighbors. Words are powerful, both for the good and the bad.

The writer of the book of James compares the power of words to bits in the mouths of horses, the rudder on a ship, and a small spark that can set a great forest on fire. He tells us that words are a restless evil, full of deadly poison that can corrupt the whole person. James 3:3-8: *"When we put bits into the mouths of horses to make them obey us, we can turn the whole animal. Or take ships as an example. Although they are so large and are driven by strong winds, they are steered by a very small rudder wherever the pilot wants to go. Likewise the tongue is a small part of the body, but it makes great boasts. Consider what a great forest is set on fire by a small spark. The tongue also is a fire, a world of evil among the parts of the body. It corrupts the whole person, sets the whole course of his life on fire, and is itself set on fire by hell. All kinds of animals, birds, reptiles and creatures of the sea are being tamed and have been tamed by man,*

The Will of God Is…

but no man can tame the tongue. It is a restless evil, full of deadly poison."

And so I will say again: From the perspective of Jesus, the number one commandment we have all broken the most, and the one we are most likely to break again, is; You shall not kill! And the weapon of choice that we use the most is words!

Don't be mistaken. Jesus knew and understood the Mosaic laws regarding the death of someone at the hands of another. He refers to those laws when he uses the word judgment in Matthew 5:21-22: *"You have heard that it was said to the people long ago, 'Do not murder, and anyone who murders will be subject to <u>judgment</u>.' But I tell you that anyone who is angry with his brother will be subject to <u>judgment</u>."* He understood the law, just as I think it might be helpful if we understand the law, in particular as it relates to: You shall not kill.

Exodus, Leviticus, Numbers, and Deuteronomy all contain the Mosaic Code of judgment for: You shall not kill. In the code there were four basic categories relating to the death of someone at the hands of another, each with their own specific set of punishments and mitigating circumstances.

1. The death of someone, the result of battle or in defense of ones life, family, and property: An early type of self-defense. 2. The death of someone, the result of prescribed punishment. 3. The death of someone, the result of fully conscious and willful intent, forethought, and planning. This is where we

get terms like malice aforethought and premeditated murder. 4. The death of someone, the result of an involuntary act or accident. It is interesting to note that the person who caused an accidental death was called the manslayer which is the origin of the contemporary legal term, manslaughter.

The death of someone, the result of willful intent, and the death of someone, the result of an involuntary act or accident, both shared similar mitigating circumstance and were subject to the same judgments. According to the Law of Moses, both types of killing were punishable by death. The person responsible for carrying out the death penalty was called the avenger or kinsman redeemer. He was the able-bodied male most closely related to the person who had been killed.

The normal means of execution were stoning, hanging on a tree, or being burned alive usually in the perpetual fires in the Valley of Ge bene Hinnom. Located outside the southwest wall of the city, the Valley of Ge bene Hinnom was used as the garbage dump for the city of Jerusalem. Refuse, waste materials, dead animals, and human corps were burned here. Fires continually smoldered, and smoke from the burning debris rose day and night. Many believe that it was from the Valley of Ge bene Hinnom that the imagery of place of eternal punishment that, "burned forever," came from. It is interesting to note that when translated into Greek, the Hebrew Valley of Ge bene Hinnom becomes

The Will of God Is...

Gehenna, which is used in the New Testament as "hell." (Matt 5:22, 5:29-30, 10:28, 18:9, 23:15, 33; Mark 9:43, 45, 47; Luke 12:5, 16:23; James 3:6, 2 Peter 2:4.

In the book of Numbers, God instructs Moses regarding how the land in Canaan will be divided up when the nation of Israel moves in following the Exodus. In chapter 35, Moses is directed to establish forty-eight cities, given specific instructions regarding the boundaries or city limits of each, and is instructed to establish among them six cities of refuge.

Here's the way it worked: If the person accused of the death of another could make it to one of these cities before the avenger could catch them, they would be given asylum. In each city there was a court of judgment made up of twenty-three non-priestly judges.

After hearing testimony, they would decide if the person was guilty or innocent. If they were found guilty, the result of willful intent, they would be turned over to the avenger to carry out the punishment. If a person was found guilty, the result of an involuntary act or accident, they were required to remain in the city of refuge until the death of the high priest.

Upon the death of the high priest, they were able to return to their home a free person. If they decided to leave the city of refuge before the high priest died, they were subject to the punishment of death by the avenger.

To make a long and getting longer story short, when Jesus said, 'Do not murder, and anyone who murders will be subject to judgment, that was the system of judgment he was referring to. The same judgment he said anyone should be subject to if they committed heart murder or tongue murder.

Heart murder is anger in our heart that becomes so all-consuming it gets in the way of our relationship with God and with others. It is an anger that causes us to step outside the protective fence of Gods love and mercy that we have surrounded ourselves with. When that happens, our anger turns into wrath, which is acted out anger, which in turn puts us in a position of vulnerability to act in such a way that becomes void of all reason and common sense and sets us up for judgment. If I have already murdered someone in my heart, then completing the job becomes much easier. That's the basis for our understanding of premeditation.

Tongue murder is anger in our heart that becomes so all-consuming it gets in the way of our relationship with God and with others. It is an anger that causes us to step outside the protective fence of Gods love and mercy that we have surrounded ourselves with. When that happens, our anger turns into wrath, which is still acted out anger, only this time it comes in the form of opening our mouth and unleashing a barrage of untrue, abusive, hurtful, and mean spirited words. Tongue murder is sometimes referred to as character assignation. If you have never been the victim of it, I can tell you from experience that you would just as soon be beaten, stabbed, or shot because the emotional pain can be as debilitating, if not more so, as the pain of a physical attack.

Jesus believed that heart murder and tongue murder were as serious, if not more, than physical murder, because in addition to setting us up for the possibility of civil judgment under the law, they could get in the way of our experiencing Sabbath.

Think about it: If you are angry with your brother and don't want to be around them, then how in heavens name can you gather together with them, in a special place, with a single focus of mind and spirit, and experience the presence of God in a way we cannot experience in any other way, at any other time, in any other place.

Therefore, Jesus says in Matthew Matt 5:23-24:"*Therefore, if you are offering your gift at the altar and there remember that your brother has something against you, leave your gift there in front of the altar. First go and be reconciled to your brother; then come and offer your gift.*"

One final point: I am not going to tell you, you shall not be angry anymore. It is too much a part of the package of emotions we have all been created with. What I will suggest is that we give serious consideration to Paul's advice to the Ephesians, 4:26-28: "*In your anger do not sin: Do not let the sun go down while you are still angry, and do not give the devil a foothold.*"

In other words, do not allow it to become so all-consuming it gets in the way of your relationship with God and with others. Don't allow it to cause you to step outside the protective fence of Gods love and mercy that you have surrounded yourself with. Don't let the sun go down while you are still angry, because if you do, it will grow and fester all night and will give the devil a foothold.

When the devil gets a foothold, it will be as though we have been handed a loaded weapon, armed with word bullets, that will wound or kill the soul and spirit of others, open the door of opportunity to all sorts of wrath, will grieve the Holy Spirit of God, and before we know it, we will once again be beating up on our self with the "what-if" stick!

Unless you are just really into the "what-if" stick thing, Paul offers an alternative: Ephesians 4:32-5:2: *"...be kind to one another, tenderhearted, forgiving one another, even as God in Christ forgave you. Therefore be imitators of God as dear children. And walk in love, as Christ also has loved us and given Himself for us...* (NKJV)

The Will of God is Be a Lover, Not a Fighter!

Nine

The Will of God is... Look the Other Way!

In chapter eight, I told you about a conversation I had a few years ago with an individual who had been beating up on herself with a "what-if" stick for over forty years. If you have ever been around anyone who is convinced that they are the worst of the worst, you know that it takes a lot to convince them that they are not. Such was the case with this individual. After my theological discourse on: You shall not kill, she replied, "well, that may be well and good but I still don't believe that you have broken all ten of the commandments." To which I again replied, "Oh yes I have!" "All ten of them?" "All ten of them!" "I know you have never committed adultery! You're a preacher." "Oh yes I have," I replied, "many times!"

You remember the survey I told you about in which the respondents were asked to rank the Ten Commandments based on the ones they had not broken or would be least likely to break? Remember

Alan Schmitt

number one on the list was you shall not kill? Guess what number two on the list was? You shall not commit adultery.

I have thought about that, and I have come to a conclusion! Those who listed: You shall not commit adultery as the number two commandment they would be least likely to break, were wrong. I would like to suggest that from the perspective of Jesus, the number two commandment we have all broken the most and the one we are most likely to break again, is; You shall not commit adultery!

The Bible teaches from beginning to end, that the sum and substance of our relationship with God and our relationship with each other is embodied in covenant relationships. Scripture and tradition make reference to three types of covenant relationships: A civil covenant: A relationship between individuals. A royal covenant: A relationship between individuals and a governing body. A divine covenant: A relationship between individuals and God.

For a covenant to be a covenant it usually has to have at least three components: 1. The terms of the covenant: What both parties of the covenant agree to do. 2. The duration of the covenant: How long it is to be honored. 3. Authentication or seal: Some type of act or gesture attesting to the agreement, by all parties, to the terms and duration of the covenant.

The original Hebrew community of believers was established through a divine covenant between

The Will of God Is…

God and Abram. (Genesis 17:1-13) The terms: God would adopt them as his children and lead them into a new land of abundance; Abram and his heirs would recognize the Lord as their only God; they would agree to follow God and to obey his word. The duration was forever, and the seal was the offering of a blood sacrifice and the mark of circumcision. From that point on, the history of the Old Testament is the history of covenants, either new ones being made or existing ones being renewed. The word testament means the witness of the covenant.

The giving of the Ten Commandments and the other laws of the Mitzvah were designed to give the covenant people of God a better understanding of his nature, and their relationship with him and each other, so that they could follow him closer, and obey his word better.

With the life, death, and resurrection of Jesus, a new covenant was made that supersedes all the earlier ones. That's why you will sometimes hear people say they are no longer living under the law. While the record of the old covenant is a valuable and essential element in our understanding of the nature of God and our relationship with him, we are living under the new covenant that God established with his people through Jesus.

The terms: God will continue to adopt them as his children. Romans 8:14-17: *"… those who are led by the Spirit of God are sons of God. For you did not receive a spirit that makes you a slave again to fear, but you received the Spirit of sonship. And by him we cry, "Abba, Father." The Spirit himself testifies with our spirit that we are God's children. Now if we are children, then we are heirs-heirs of God and co-heirs with Christ,"*

His people will recognize the Lord as their only God, and Jesus Christ as his son, and agree to follow him, and obey his word. Romans 10:9: *"... if you confess with your mouth, "Jesus is Lord," and believe in your heart that God raised him from the dead, you will be saved."*

The duration is forever, and the seal was the offering of a blood sacrifice in the person of Jesus. John 3:16: *"For God so loved the world that he gave his one and only Son, that whoever believes in him shall not perish but have eternal life."*

When you think about it, the history of our lives is a history of covenants. The one covenant that I believe is next in line in importance to our covenant relationship with God is the covenant relationship we make in marriage. I think that may be why Matthew records Jesus electing to use the only one of the Ten Commandments that relates to the marriage covenant as the framework to give the disciples insight into the importance of all covenant relationships. He knew that they knew the importance of the marriage covenant.

A marriage is a covenant relationship. Everything in a wedding is by design, a symbol of a covenant

The Will of God Is...

between two people. I have a wedding resource notebook that has seventy different kinds of wedding vows. Some are very traditional dating back to the 1662 Book of Common Prayer and many are more contemporary in nature. The one thing they all have in common is their declaration that in a marriage, a covenant relationship is being created.

Let's use the old traditional vows as an example, and I will use it, for our purposes here, from the perspective of the groom, although it is the same for the bride: Forty-four years ago I said, *I Alan, take you Saundra to be my wedded wife*. With that, the principles in the relationship are identified and the purpose of the covenant is established.

Now come the conditions. *To have and to hold from this day forward:* I receive you today as a part of who I am and to hold on to you forever, regardless of whether or not that forever includes better or worse – richer or poorer – in sickness and in health – It doesn't matter because I covenant today to love and to cherish you... Now comes the duration of the covenant: *till death us do part*.

The vows are then followed by the seal of the covenant: The wedding Rings. *The wedding ring is the outward and visible sign of an inward and spiritual grace, signifying the uniting of this man and woman in the covenant relationship of matrimony.*

Now, how does all this relate to: You shall not commit adultery? God tells the community of believers that he is the Lord their God and that they are to have no other gods before or beside him. Do not allow anything or anybody to become more important than God. Do not allow anything or anybody to become as important as God. If you do, then that anything or that anybody becomes an idol and your commitment or devotion to them becomes idolatry. When you become committed and devoted to an idol, you cease to be committed and devoted to God.

When you cease to be committed and devoted to God, you become unfaithful to your covenant relationship with him. When you become unfaithful to that covenant relationship, your relationship with God becomes an adulteress relationship, because adultery means unfaithfulness to a covenant.

In the same way, if you have ever allowed anything or anybody to become more important than your spouse; If you have ever allowed anything to become of equal importance to your spouse, from the perspective of Jesus, you have committed adultery without ever coming close to violating the sanctity of the intimacy of marriage. If you have ever allowed anything or anybody to get in the way of you fulfilling the terms of your marriage relationship you have committed adultery.

One of the most potentially destructive examples of my committing adultery was in the late 1970's and early 1980's, when I first went into the ministry. I was young, ambitious, believed that the Lord had called me to save the world at any cost. Within a year I was committing adultery. You could probably say I was having an affair. You could probably go as far as saying I had a mistress. She was a holy mistress.

She was the church! For you see, in less than a year, I allowed serving the church to become more important than my relationship with the Lord, and more important than my relationship with my wife. Ever heard the term, "Married to your job?"

Nine years ago, when I felt the call of the Lord to return to the pulpit ministry, my number one concern was the potential for slipping back into an adulteress relationship with my old holy mistress. While the temptation has been there many times, thankfully I have been able to resist.

In Matthew 5:29-30, I believe Jesus is attempting to convey to the disciples how serious unfaithfulness to a covenant is: *"If your right eye causes you to sin, gouge it out and throw it away. It is better for you to lose one part of your body than for your whole body to be thrown into hell. And if your right hand causes you to sin, cut it off and throw it away. It is better for you to lose one part of your body than for your whole body to go into hell."* If you're right eye or right hand causes you to sin, - and the implication here is that the sin he is referring to is adultery - gouge it out, cut it off, and throw it away. It is better for you to lose one part of your body than for your whole body to be thrown into hell.

Every time I read that passage I am reminded of how thankful I am that our culture doesn't follow it literally. From the perspective of Jesus, if we did, there would be a lot of visually impaired and physically handicapped people in our world, including me.

One final point: How do we defend ourselves against all the things and people in the world that represent the potential for us to commit adultery? That which works best for me is simply to look the other way! When I see something that I know represents the potential for me to commit adultery in my mind, my heart, or my actions, I try to look the other way. Rather than allowing my attention and focus to become fixed on the temptation that is before me, I try to fix my eyes on Jesus, the author and perfector of my faith. I like the way the Message says it: Hebrews 12:2-3:

"Keep your eyes on Jesus, who both began and finished this race we're in. Study how he did it. Because he never lost sight of where he was headed — that exhilarating finish in and with God — he could put up with anything along the way: cross, shame, whatever. And now he's there, in the place of honor, right alongside God. When you find yourselves flagging in your faith, go over that story again, item by item, that long litany of hostility he plowed through. That will shoot adrenaline into your souls!" (MSG)

The Will of God is Look the Other way.

Ten

The Will of God is...
Don't Steal Anything!

His name was Carl. He was a classmate in Junior High School. One Saturday afternoon, when I was hanging out over at his house trying to make time with his sister, his dad asked us to go to the hardware store and buy him some coarse grade steel wool. He gave us the money and off we went.

On our way, we came up with what we thought was an excellent plan to make some money off our errand. If we could steal the steel wool from the hardware store, Carl could use part of the money to buy some smokes and I could use my share to make some major points with his sister over at the A & W Root Beer stand. Our plan was simple. While he was talking to the store clerk, I would slip the package of steel wool down my pants. It was a great plan and it worked, except for one thing. The steel wool was unwrapped. If you have never stuck an unwrapped bundle of coarse steel wool down your pants, trust me you don't want to do it.

By the time we got back to his house, I was itching so bad I had to go home. If that wasn't bad enough, when I got home, I had to explain to my mom why I needed the whole bottle of calamine lotion and why I needed it where I needed it! To make matters worse, Carl kept all the money, and I made zero points with his sister at the A & W! When I walked out of that hardware store, I was a thief and had broken the eighth commandment for the first time in my life.

His name was Ronnie. He was seven years old and in the second grade. At the annual parent-teacher conference, Ronnie's mother told his teacher that he was an unwanted mistake, was nothing but trouble, would never be as good as his sister, and would never amount to anything.

She told her all of this while Ronnie was sitting there listening to it. Guess what? Ronnie was nothing but trouble, a teacher's nightmare! When I had him in class, he got mad at me about something and broke my car window in retaliation. He has never amounted to anything and today, Ronnie is in prison. When his mother walked out of his second grade class room that night, she was a thief and had broken the eighth commandment in a brutal and vicious way.

From as far back as she could remember, her daddy was mean to her and would do things to her that he didn't do to her sisters. He would do things to her that hurt and made her cry. She would wonder: why does daddy hug my sisters and hit me? The more pain she felt, the more she withdrew into the protective world of an emotional shell.

When I first met her some twenty-five years later, she was so deep inside that shell I wasn't sure anything or anybody would ever be able to get her to open up and come out. Her daddy was a thief of the worst kind, and he too broke the eighth commandment in a brutal and vicious way.

They were an established church that had been in the neighborhood for well over a hundred years. They were satisfied and comfortable in how they worshiped and did ministry, because they had been satisfied and comfortable in how they worshiped and did ministry for a long time. They saw no need or good reason to change the status quo way they did worship and ministry.

One day they were given the opportunity to do ministry in a new and different way. Their response to this new and wonderful opportunity for making disciples of Jesus Christ was a resounding, resentful, and rebellious no! "We have never done it that way before and we're not about to start now. If they want to worship and do ministry like that, then they need to go to another church." With each resounding, resentful, and rebellious no that was said or acted out, they broke the eighth commandment in a way that was contrary to the very gospel they were supposed to be preaching, teaching, and living out in their lives.

"A young child asked his mother, who is God? And his mother answered, eat your supper. A young child asked his father, who is God? And his father answered, do your chores. A young child asked his teacher, who is God? His teacher answered, do your homework. A young child asks his pastor, who is God? His pastor answered, read the Bible. Pretty soon, the young child didn't ask anymore, who is God?"[3] Do you see it? A mother, a father, a teacher, and a pastor all broke the eighth commandment.

Have you grown up thinking, you shall not steal simply meant you shall not steal stuff? I would like to propose to you that the Will of God is don't steal anything!

In the historical context of the early community of believers, stealing and the laws that applied to stealing had to do with stuff. In particular, property that included land, animals, slaves, and family, the most valuable of which was a man's animals.

In Old Testament law, there were two common categories of offenders: One was someone who would sneak in and steal without the owner knowing it at the time. The other was one who would take the property of another, face to face, often using force to do it.

The typical punishments for breaking the laws against stealing were some sort of restitution. For example, it you were caught with the property of another, the punishment would be to repay double

The Will of God Is...

the value of what was taken. If a stolen animal was sold or slaughtered, additional punishments would be required. For a sold or slaughtered sheep, the punishment was to repay four times the value of what was taken. For a sold or slaughtered oxen, it was five times the value, because if a farmer had no oxen, he could not plow.

If the perpetrator was unable to pay, they were sold into slavery with the proceeds of their sale going to help pay their restitution. They remained in slavery until total repayment was made which, if one was a slave, meant never. If a person killed someone in the act of stealing, they would be subject to the standard punishments for murder. When the scripture tells us that the two who were crucified with Jesus were thieves, it is generally understood that they were being put to death because they had killed someone in the act of robbing them.

In the historical context of the early community of believers, stealing and the laws that applied to stealing had to do with property: Simple, to the point, with little or no interpretation necessary. You shall not steal another person's property. If you do, pay the fine, accept the punishment, and that's it.

I have thought about that, and I have struggled with it. Like murder and adultery, if Jesus had elected to use, "do not steal" as an example of how we could transform an impersonal law prohibiting the taking of someone's sheep or oxen, into an attitude of the heart, how would he have done it?

Here's what I have come up with. Two conclusions: 1. A person's property is more than just the tangibles of physical property. 2. The creative ways we commit heart murder, tongue murder, and adultery, are equally matched with the ways we steal.

Mark 12:28-30: *"One of the teachers of the law came and heard them debating. Noticing that Jesus had given them a good answer, he asked him, 'Of all the commandments, which is the most important?' 'The most important one,' answered Jesus, 'is this: 'Hear, O Israel, the Lord our God, the Lord is one. Love the Lord your God with all your heart and with all your soul and with all your mind and with all your strength.'"*

In reading that passage, have you ever wondered why Jesus didn't just say: Love the Lord your God with your total being? Why did he specifically divide one's total being into heart, soul, mind, and strength? You suppose his response was a reflection of his understanding of our human nature?

Consider this: Who we are is the sum of what we possess. Heart, mind, soul, and strength are the individual properties that comprise who we are. From a biblical perspective, our strength represents our physical attributes and abilities. The tangibles of who we are. Our physical property. Our mind is our intellectual attributes and abilities. Our ability to think and reason; the process of dreaming, creating, and understanding. Our intellectual property.

The Will of God Is...

Our soul is our point of contact with God. The conduit for us to receive and experience the presence and power of the Holy Spirit in our lives. The door into which God is able to enter our lives. Our spiritual property.

From a biblical perspective, our heart represents our ability to feel, our ability to express our feelings, our human reservoir of love and compassion. Our emotional property.

The Will of God is don't steal anything: Don't steal another person's physical property, their intellectual property, their spiritual property, or their emotional property.

Do you see it? Do you see how a mother in a second grade classroom could be a thief? She stole the dreams, the creative excitement of life from a little seven-year-old boy. She stole his ability to feel, especially the love and compassion from the one person he needed to feel it from the most.

You see how an abusive father could be a thief of the worst kind, forcing a little girl into being a prisoner in an emotional shell, the victim of emotional theft and vandalism.

You see how people in a church can become a gang of thieves and violate the Will of God in way that is contrary to the very gospel they are supposed to be preaching, teaching, and living out in their lives. People like the Romans Paul was writing to when he said, *"You who preach against stealing, do you steal? You who say that people should not commit adultery, do you commit adultery? You who abhor idols, do you rob temples? You who brag about the law, do you dishonor God by breaking the law?"* (Romans 2:21-24 :)

Surely, we're not like them, are we? Surely, we have never dishonored God by breaking the law, have we? Surely, none of us have ever said anything or done anything that has robbed someone of their physical property, their intellectual property, their spiritual property, or their emotional property?

If by chance you have, then I would like to encourage you to begin the process of restitution immediately. A process of restitution called forgiveness. You can ask God to forgive you seventy times seven different times, in seventy times seven different ways and you will still owe on your restitution. For you see, it is not until you ask for forgiveness of your trespasses from the one you have trespassed against, that your restitution will be complete.

The Will of God is Don't Steal Anything!

Eleven

The Will of God is... Let Your Yes be Yes and Your No be No!

Do you solemnly swear to tell the truth, the whole truth, and nothing but the truth, so help you God? Have you ever made that oath?

How about this one? Do you truly and earnestly repent of your sins, accept Jesus Christ as your Lord and Savior, and pledge your allegiance to his kingdom? Do you receive and profess the Christian faith as contained in the scriptures of the Old and New Testaments? Do you promise according to the grace given you to live a Christian life, obediently keep God's holy will and commandments, and always remain a faithful member of Christ's holy Church? Have you ever made that oath? If you have, then I would propose that you have made the first one as well.

When we accept Jesus Christ as our Savior, I believe we solemnly swear to tell the truth, the whole truth, and nothing but the truth, because the Jesus we accept is the embodiment of the God of truth. Jesus characterized himself as the truth. No one can understand the truth about the nature of the Father except by understanding the nature of the Son. John 14:6-7: *"I am the way and the <u>truth</u> and the life. No one comes to the Father except through me. If you really knew me, you would know my Father as well. From now on, you do know him and have seen him."*

When we profess the Christian faith as contained in the scriptures of the Old and New Testaments, I believe we solemnly swear to tell the truth, the whole truth, and nothing but the truth, because scripture is the recorded Word of God, our textbook for living. When we read the scripture it is as though God himself is teaching a class on discipleship. John 8:31-32: *"Jesus said, 'If you hold to my teaching, you are really my disciples. Then you will know the truth, and the truth will set you free.'"*

When we promise to live a Christian life and always remain a faithful member of Christ's holy church, I believe we solemnly swear to tell the truth, the whole truth, and nothing but the truth, because we make an oath to open the door of our life to the guiding, sustaining, and empowering presence and power of the Holy Spirit, the very presence of God who Jesus calls the Spirit of Truth. John 16:13: *"But when he, the Spirit of truth, comes, he will guide you into all truth."*

When we promise to obediently keep God's holy will and commandments, I believe we solemnly

The Will of God Is...

swear to tell the truth, the whole truth, and nothing but the truth, because God's holy will is embodied in his holy commandments, number nine of which says, You shall not give false testimony against your neighbor!

In chapters nine & ten, I made reference to a survey in which the respondents were asked to rank the Ten Commandments, from one to ten, based on the ones they had not broken or would be least likely to break? Number one on the list was, "You shall not kill." Number two on the list was, "You shall not commit adultery." Number ten on the list? The majority of respondents said that the commandment they have broken the most and the one they would be most likely to break again is: You shall not give false testimony against your neighbor!

In the comments section, the consensus was that there is little guilt or remorse in violating the ninth commandment because violating it is not as serious or harmful as the others. Honesty is no longer the only or best policy. It is now simply considered to be one of many options, along with dishonesty, that are acceptable and commonly use as tools to accomplish a particular purpose or agenda: A classic example of the ends justifying the means.

In its historical context, the ninth commandment was related to religious and civil law in which witnesses and their testimony were required in order to render a legal judgment. According to the Mosaic Code, conviction of serious crimes required two or more witnesses. Deuteronomy 19:15: *"One witness is not enough to convict a man accused of any crime or offense he may have committed. A matter must be established by the testimony of two or three witnesses."*

In order to ensure that the testimony would be the truth, the whole truth, and nothing but the truth, witnesses were required to make a solemn statement or claim as a means of validating their promise to tell the truth. These solemn statements were known as an oath.

Oaths were often accompanied by some symbolic gesture such as raising the hand (Gen 14:22), laying their hands on the head of the accused (Lev. 24:14), and a male touching his genitals (Gen. 24:2). It is from this practice that we get the term testimony, which means the content of a witness statement.

Oaths were serious business. There are a number of instances recorded in scripture when the one giving the oath would include some sort of self-imposed curse if they didn't tell the truth. A kind of, "cross my heart, hope to die, stick a million needles in my eye," if I don't tell the truth curse. Oaths were serious business, because in swearing a solemn statement, the witness was charged not only by the court to tell the truth, but also by God himself.

When we say, I swear to tell the truth, the whole truth, and nothing but the truth, so help me God, we are using the authority of God's name as verification of our truthfulness to the court while

The Will of God Is...

at the same time we are also making an oath to God that we will be truthful. Consequently, if our testimony is not true, we are not only in violation of commandment nine, we have misused the name of the Lord and are also in violation of the second commandment. We see this reflected in Lev 19:12: *"'Do not swear falsely by my name and so profane the name of your God."*

Oaths were serious business. If the witness was found to be bearing false testimony, their punishment would be to receive the same penalty as the accused. Deuteronomy 19:16-21: *"If a malicious witness takes the stand to accuse a man of a crime, the two men involved in the dispute must stand in the presence of the Lord before the priests and the judges who are in office at the time. The judges must make a thorough investigation, and if the witness proves to be a liar, giving false testimony against his brother, then do to him as he intended to do to his brother. You must purge the evil from among you - which is where the term perjury comes from - The rest of the people will hear of this and be afraid, and never again will such an evil thing be done among you. Show no pity: life for life, eye for eye, tooth for tooth, hand for hand, foot for foot."*

Oaths were serious business. If the witness was found to be bearing false testimony, not only were they in violation of commandment nine, not only were they were guilty of misusing the name of the Lord their God, commandment two, but according to Jeremiah, they were guilty of violating the fourth commandment and were not worthy to enter the presence of the Lord and experience Sabbath. Jeremiah 7:2-11: *"Hear the word of the Lord, all you people of Judah who come through these gates to worship the Lord. This is what the Lord Almighty, the God of Israel, says: Reform your ways and your actions, and I will let you live in this place. 4 Do not trust in deceptive words and say, 'This is the temple of the Lord, the temple of the Lord, the temple of the Lord!' If you really change your ways and your actions and deal with each other justly, if you do not oppress the alien, the fatherless or the widow and do not shed innocent blood in this place, and if you do not follow other gods to your own harm, then I will let you live in this place, in the land I gave your forefathers for ever and ever. But look, you are trusting in deceptive words that are worthless. 'Will you steal and murder, commit adultery and perjury, burn incense to Baal and follow other gods you have not known, and then come and stand before me in this house, which bears my Name, and say, We are safe--safe to do all these detestable things?' Has this house, which bears my Name, become a den of robbers to you?'"*

Oaths were serious business because the level of importance they placed on honesty in the courtroom was an extension of the level of importance that was placed on honesty outside the courtroom as well. Do you solemnly swear to tell the truth, the whole truth, and nothing but the truth, so help you God, was supposed to be an unwritten rule of life as well as the rule of law. That is how I see the ninth commandment fit into the overall package of the Will of God.

I believe that is what Jesus was saying in Matt 5:34:*"But I tell you, Do not swear at all"* He wasn't saying not to follow the rule of law as much as he was teaching the disciples, present company included, that their life should be an oath in action.

When we accept Jesus Christ as our Savior, our lives should say I solemnly swear to tell the truth, the whole truth, and nothing but the truth, because the Jesus I accept is the embodiment of the God of truth.

When we profess the Christian faith as contained in the scriptures of the Old and New Testaments, our lives should be tangible evidence that we know the truth, that the truth has set us free, and that we solemnly swear to tell the truth, the whole and nothing but the truth.

When we promise to live a Christian life and always remain a faithful member of Christ's holy church, then our lives should be a living testimony that we are connected to the guiding, sustaining, and empowering presence and power of the Holy Spirit, the very presence of God who Jesus calls the Spirit of Truth.

When we promise to obediently keep God's holy will and commandments, our Yes should be Yes, and our No should be No, because as John writes,

We know that we have come to know him if we obey his commands. The man who says, "I know him," but does not do what he commands is a liar, and the truth is not in him.

When we attempt to live a life that says, I solemnly swear to tell the truth, the whole and nothing but the truth, so help me God, I believe the most important element in that oath is the phrase, so help me God.

If, when we accept Jesus as our Lord and Savior, we truly profess and promise to walk as he walked, to live our life as an oath in action, then I believe the number one prayer on our daily prayer list must be, help me God!

I want to conclude this chapter by asking you to repeat the following oath. It doesn't matter what your denominational connection may be. It is an oath that applies to all Christians. It's a big deal, so make it a big deal! Stand up and read the question and your response out loud.

Do you truly and earnestly repent of your sins, accept Jesus Christ as your Lord and Savior, and pledge your allegiance to his kingdom?
I Do!

Do you receive and profess the Christian faith as contained in the scriptures of the Old and New Testaments?
I Do!

The Will of God Is…

Do you promise according to the grace given you to live a Christian life, obediently keep God's holy will and commandments, and always remain a faithful member of Christ's Holy Church?
I Do!

Do you solemnly swear that the testimony you have just given is the truth, the whole truth, and nothing but the truth, so help you God?
I Do!

One final point: As you leave this chapter, please remember: You are under oath!

The Will of God is Let Your Yes be Yes and Your No be No!

Twelve

The Will of God is...
Don't Let What Others Have, Get in the Way of What you have!

When I was teaching school, I would do a unit each year in my Psychology class on anger. I would begin by asking the question: What makes you angry? I would then list their answers on the chalkboard. When the answers stopped or the board was full, we would then explore why each thing they had listed made them angry. I did this for ten years and every class came to the same conclusion. The overwhelming, some would say the only; reason we get angry is because we do not get our own way.

We get angry, heated, up in arms, infuriated, chafed, fuming, boiling, enraged, miffed, incensed, etc., etc., in one way or another, when we do not get what we want; we do not get what we want when or how or in the manner we want it; or we do not get what we want to happen to the person or persons we want it to happen to, good or bad!

The Will of God Is...

Some would say even righteous anger - getting angry for the cause of right, goodness, and justice - has as its source, our not getting what we want; when or how or in the manner we want it, or to the person or persons we want it to happen to.

The next step in our survey on anger was to list some of the things our anger causes us to do. Some of the responses listed by the students were: Lose control. Do not exercise good judgment. Do and say stupid things. Do and say painful things. Do and say things that we shouldn't or wouldn't do or say under normal circumstances. Do and say and think things we know are wrong, but we do them anyway and then try to justify them as being ok. Then we find ourselves having to do damage control – If we are lucky, apologizing, eating humble pie, or asking for forgiveness will do the job.

Sometimes, however, damage control can be very painful to us and the ones we have leveled our anger against. Sometimes, it even costs us our freedom, our lives, the lives of those we love, and sometimes the lives of innocent people.

At the beginning of our examination of the Ten Commandments as the pre-destined will of God, I suggested that the first four commandments provide insight and direction regarding the nature of God and what he expects our relationship to Him to be. The remaining six are designed to give us insight and direction into what He expects our relationship with others to be. All of which are the basic foundational principles of the people of God that are taught and re-taught throughout the rest of scripture, both Old and New Testament.

Through the pages of this book, I believe we have found that all ten of them do that by either telling us what we should do, or what we shouldn't do.

Therefore, I would like to propose that you shall not covet is where it is in the order of commandments, number ten of ten, because it serves as a summary of the other nine and, in particular, gives us some insights into why we don't do what we should do, and why we do what we shouldn't do.

You shall not covet... the possessions (house), family (wife), or livelihood (servants, ox, donkey) – that belongs to your neighbor. Neighbor in this context means the entire community of faith, not just the one you may be living next door to. There are a number of adjectives in the scripture that are used interchangeably with the word covet, including greed, envy, or desire. As I understand these terms and how they relate to each other, there appears to be a pecking order of sorts.

It begins with a harmless desire. We think about how nice something is that someone else has and wish we could have it. The desire doesn't last long, usually because we are able to justify why we don't want it or don't need it.

If it doesn't stop there, then it moves up a notch to envy. Envy is when we begin to transform our harmless desire to have something, into what we perceive as a need to have it. We then begin to develop a feeling of resentment and jealousy toward the person or persons who have it. We now find it easy to justify why they don't deserve it and why we should have it. You know what resentment is? It's anger on simmer.

If envy is allowed to fester without treatment, it eventually will graduate to covet or covetousness. Covetousness will then trigger our inherent human attitude of greed. When greed is in control long enough, it will begin turning up the burner under the anger pot from resentment to wrath. In the context of the scripture, wrath means anger acted out.

Do you see it? What started out as a harmless desire for something has become an all consuming potentially destructive obsession to have something that someone else has, whatever the costs. We get angry, heated, up in arms, infuriated, chafed, fuming, boiling, enraged, miffed, incensed in one way or another, when we do not get what we want; we do not get what we want when or how or in the manner we want it, or we do not get what we want to happen to the person or persons we want it to happen to.

We lose control. Do not exercise good judgment. Do and say stupid things. Do and say painful things. Do and say things that we shouldn't or wouldn't do under normal circumstances. Do and say and think things we know are wrong, but we do them anyway and then try to justify them as being ok.

It is at that point that we allow what others have to get in the way of what we have. We begin to allow what it is that we want or our resentment toward the person who has it. It then becomes more important than our relationship with God and others, or of equal importance to our relationship with God and others, and thus violate commandment number one.

Or how about allowing what it is that we want or our resentment toward the person who has it to so consume us that it becomes the object of our total focus, commitment, and dependence: a violation of commandment number two. Ephesians 5:5: *"For of this you can be sure: No immoral, impure or greedy person-such a man is an idolater-has any inheritance in the kingdom of Christ and of God."*

We lose control, do not exercise good judgment, do and say painful things. Do and say things that we shouldn't or wouldn't do under normal circumstances. Like misusing the name and authority of God to justify our actions, and thus violate commandment number three. "God spoke to me and told me to act this way!" Well, maybe he did and maybe he didn't. How do we know? I have found that one good rule of thumb to follow in deciding if it is God speaking is this: God doesn't speak stupid. We do and then give him the credit!

How about deceiving ourselves into thinking that devoting our time and attention to getting what we want is more important than taking time out to gather together, in a special place, with a single focus of mind and spirit, and experience the presence of God in a way we cannot experience in any other way, at any other time, in any other place, and thus violating commandment number four.

When we turn up the burner under the anger pot from resentment to wrath and allow what started out as a harmless desire for something to become an all consuming potentially destructive obsession to have something that someone else has, what ever the cost, we then set the stage for hurting and dishonoring our family, our neighbors, our friends, even to the extent of committing murder, adultery, becoming a thief, and a liar.

Doing and saying things that can be very painful to us and the ones we have leveled our anger against. Doing and saying things that can sometimes cost us our freedom, our lives, the lives of those we love, and sometimes the lives of innocent people. In the process, we violate commandments five, six, seven, eight, and nine, all because we didn't get our own way and didn't have sense enough to put out the brush fire in our relationship with God and others before it becomes a raging forest fire.

How do we keep a simple desire from becoming obsessive covetousness greed? How about by focusing on what we have, rather than on what we don't have. How about replacing our envy, resentment, and anger with thanksgiving?

I am thankful for the wife who says its hot dogs tonight, because she is home with me, not with someone else.

I am thankful for the teenager who is complaining about doing dishes, because that means he or she is at home and not on the streets.

I am thankful for the taxes I pay, because that means I am employed.

I am thankful for the clothes that fit a little too snug, because it means I have enough to eat.

I am thankful for the lawn that needs mowing, windows that need cleaning, and gutters that need fixing, because it means I have a home.

I am thankful for my huge heating bill, because it means I am warm.

I am thankful for folks that may get a little too noisy in church, because it means I can hear.

I am thankful for the pile of laundry and ironing, because it means I have clothes to wear.

I am thankful for the alarm that goes off in the early morning hours, because it means that I am alive.

I am thankful for the disagreements I have with my friends, because it means I have friends willing to disagree with me.

"I bet you have never broken all ten of the commandments! Oh yes I have, I replied! All ten of them? All ten of them! Yes, I have broken all ten of them and chances are good that I will break one of more of them again. But, here is the good news of the Good News: *"But in our time something new has been added. What Moses and the prophets witnessed to all those years has happened. The God-setting-things-right that we read about has*

The Will of God Is...

become Jesus-setting-things-right for us. And not only for us, but for everyone who believes in him. For there is no difference between us and them in this. Since we've compiled this long and sorry record as sinners (both us and them) and proved that we are utterly incapable of living the glorious lives God wills for us, God did it for us. Out of sheer generosity he put us in right standing with himself. A pure gift. He got us out of the mess we're in and restored us to where he always wanted us to be. And he did it by means of Jesus Christ. God sacrificed Jesus on the altar of the world to clear that world of sin. Having faith in him sets us in the clear. God decided on this course of action in full view of the public—to set the world in the clear with himself through the sacrifice of Jesus, finally taking care of the sins he had so patiently endured. This is not only clear, but it's now—this is current history! God sets things right. He also makes it possible for us to live in his rightness." Romans 3:21-26 (MSG)

One final point: You suppose it would be too much of a stretch to suggest that this commandment might be applicable in the reverse? In addition to don't let what others have, get in the way of what you have, how about don't intentionally say or do anything that will cause others to let what you have, get in the way of what they have.

The Will of God is, Don't Let What Others Have get in the Way of What You Have!

Epilogue

The Will of God is... God's Will or My Will? An interview with God

When I first preached the content of this book as a series of sermons, I asked the congregation to help me write the final message with any unanswered questions they still had regarding the Will of God. I received one response. Ironically, the same question that served as the motivation to do the Will of God series in the first place: How do I know if something is God's will or my will?

Based of what we have discovered and affirmed on our discernment journey, I would like to attempt an answer to that question, in the form of an interview with God. An imaginary face to face meeting with God in which he is asked the question: Is what I want to do your will or my will?

God: Good morning Leeman.
Lee: Good morning Father. Thank you for taking the time to visit with me.

God: Not a problem. Nothing gives me greater joy than to talk with my children. You know it wouldn't hurt you to do it more often.

Lee: I know Father. Please forgive me.

God: It wouldn't hurt if you asked me that more often, too.

Lee: Yes sir.

God: You know I am serious about forgiveness, Leeman; Just ask my Son.

Lee: Father, with all due respect, I really don't like you calling me Leeman.
When I was growing up, the only time I heard Leeman was when I was in trouble. Can we just stick with Lee?

God: Sure Lee. I am sorry for making you feel uncomfortable. Will you forgive me?

Lee: Yes sir.

God: While we are on the subject, how are you doing in forgiving others?

Lee: Would it be okay if we changed the subject?

God: I knew you were going to say that! Okay, what can I do for you?

Lee: Well Father, you know I am 66 years old…

God: You want to try again?

Lee: Okay, 68. How did you know that? Never mind! Anyway, I have always wanted to own a black BMW convertible with tan leather interior.

God: You talking about the M6 or the V4 model?

Lee: The M6.

God: Sweet! So, are you looking at the premium package, with the 5.0 liter, 10 valve, overhead cam engine?

Lee: Yes sir.

God: The seven-speed semi-automatic transmission?

Lee: Yes sir.

God: Awesome!

Lee: How do you know so much about BMW's? Oh yea! You're God.

God: So what does your wanting to buy a BMW have to do with me?

Lee: I want to know if it is your will or my will?

God: My will? Why would I want a BMW convertible? I don't have time to drive one, and anyway, have you seen the price of gasoline? It's okay Lee.
Your question is one I am asked quite often. I am just surprised that you would be asking it? Did you know that it was a question like that that inspired your pastor to do a series on my will? You have been listening to his sermons haven't you?

Lee: Yes sir, I faithfully listen to every word he says every Sunday!

God: Really?

Lee: Well most of the time.

God: Here's how it works. When I put this creation thing all together, I gave you free will. You know what that means?

Lee: I think so, but I have never heard it from you?

God: Free will means I have given you the ability to make decisions for yourself. I decided from the start that I was not going to micro-manage my creation. That's why our relationship has been characterized as that of a loving father and his children: A relationship in which your heavenly father allows you to make decisions for yourself.

Lee: Yes sir, I think so.

God: Let me put it this way. Do you love your children? Have they ever made decisions that you were proud of?

Lee: Yes sir.

God: Have they ever made decisions that you didn't like or approve of? Have their decisions ever hurt you? Have you ever had to do damage control because of their misguided choices?

Lee: Yes sir.

God: Do you love them any more or any less because of the decisions they make?

Lee: No sir.

God: Does that answer your question?

Lee: Yes sir. I am sorry for the decisions I have made in my life that have not been pleasing to you Father.

God: Me too Lee, but that's okay because you are still my son and I still love you.

God: Lee, what I think you are asking about the BMW is whether or not your purchase of it will get in the way of our relationship. Will the new car cause you to veer away from my predestined will for you?

Lee: I never thought of it that way.

God: Are you familiar with Isaiah 1:18?

Lee: No sir.

God: It's the one that says: "Come now, let us reason together," says me.

Lee: Sounds familiar.

God: How about we do a little reasoning together?

Lee: What do you mean?

God: Let me ask you some questions, okay?

Lee: Okay.

God: Question number one: Do you swear that the answers you are about to give are the truth, the whole truth, and nothing but the truth, so help you me?

Lee: Why are you asking me that?

God: Because your answers to the rest of my questions will be useless if you will not first agree to be truthful with me. You are always truthful, aren't you Lee?

Lee: Oh, yes sir!

God: Always? With everyone?

Lee: I swear that the answers I am about to give you are the truth, the whole truth, and nothing but the truth, so help me you!

God: Okay. Next, will you allow your new car to become more important, or of equal importance to me and our relationship?

Lee: No sir!

God: Will you allow the car to become the object of your total focus and devotion?
Lee: You mean like an idol?
God: Yes.
Lee: No sir, never!
God: Will purchasing the car or owning the car cause you to misuse or abuse my name?
Lee: Absolutely not Father. When I pray, "Hallowed be Thy name…" I mean what I say!
God: How about when you were working on your back porch and you cut that trim board too short?
Lee: You heard that?
God: What do you think?
Lee: Well, you know it just slipped out.
God: Well, you know it doesn't matter how it got out, when you said it you hurt me.
Lee: Sorry!
God: Where are you going to park the car on Sunday morning?
Lee: What?
God: Where are you going to park the car on Sunday morning?
Lee: Where am I going to park the car on Sunday morning? *(pause)* Oh I know! I'm going to park it on the church parking lot.
God: Why on the church parking lot?
Lee: Because I will be inside for Sabbath.
God: Good! Okay. Now let's talk about your family. How does Kay feel about you purchasing the car?

Lee: She's okay with it.

God: That's not what I heard the other day when you first brought it up.

Lee: You don't miss anything do you?

God: So, how is purchasing the car going to affect your relationship with Kay?
You know this family thing is very important to me!

Lee: While not as excited as I am, she can live with it! She has seen it, driven it; we have run the figures over and over, and she is really excited about it. She's looking forward to evening drives with the top down; parking by the lake under the moon light, if you know what I mean?

God: I get the picture! Next question: In order to purchase your new car, will you commit heart murder or tongue murder?

Lee: I remember Pastor Alan going over those, but could you give me a quick review?

God: Heart murder is anger in your heart that becomes so all-consuming it causes you to do things that get in the way of your relationship with me and with others. You've had experience with this one Lee.

Lee: I was afraid you would bring that up.

God: You know what can happen! Your anger turns into wrath, which is acted out anger, which in turn puts you in a position of vulnerability to act in such a way that becomes void of all reason and common sense. You ever acted in a way that is void of all reason and common sense?

Lee: Do I have to answer that one?

God: Tongue murder is like heart murder; It is anger in your heart that becomes so all-consuming that your words get in the way of your relationship with God and with others. This one ring a bell with you?

Lee: Oh yes! My tongue has got me in trouble many times!

God: How about 416,793 times?

Lee: Yes sir!

God Next question: Will your new car cause you to commit adultery?

Lee: Adultery? Absolutely not! I have been a faithful husband for almost 46 years! I would never allow anything to come between me and Kay.

God: What about between you and me?

Lee: What do you mean?

God: When you cease to be committed and devoted to me, you become unfaithful to your covenant relationship with me. When that happens, your relationship with me becomes an adulteress relationship. Look, for me, our relationship is much more that a casual acquaintance. It is the real deal!

Lee: Yes sir.

God: How would you feel if you discovered Kay was unfaithful to your marriage covenant?

Lee: I would be angry, hurt, disappointed... *(pause)* like you get when I am unfaithful to my covenant with you?

God: So what about the car? You going to let it become your mistress?

Lee: No sir!

God: Are you going to flaunt the car and make others feel jealous?

Lee: What do you mean?

God: Will you say or do anything that will cause others to let what you have, get in the way of what they have?

Lee: You mean like me cause them to covet my car?

God: Yes

Lee: You know, I have never thought of it that way. It makes sense. I should not say or do anything that will cause others to let what I have, get in the way of what they have? Now that I know that can happen Father, I will try not to let it happen.

God: Good. I think you are starting to understand. We're about finished.
What's the MSRP on the new car?

Lee: $82,000.00.

God: You going to pay cash or finance it?

Lee: Finance.

God: How long?

Lee: Three years.

God: You know that's $2,277.77 a month, without interest?

Lee: Yes sir.

God: What are you going to steal to come up with that kind of money?

Lee: Steal? Listen, I may be guilty of a lot of things but I am not a thief!

God: Really? Tell me: Is the stress from that kind of financial obligation going to affect your health? What about Kay? You know how stress affects her diabetes. If it does Lee, that's stealing from your quality of life to get what you want. Is the demand to meet that kind of financial obligation going to preoccupy you mind so much that there won't be any room left for other things or other people? If it does, you will be stealing from your relationship with your friends, your neighbors, and your church family.

Speaking of your church family: is that kind of financial obligation going to affect your relationship with your church family, your commitment to the church's vision for ministry? Is that kind of financial obligation going to affect your financial commitment to the church? You know they are depending on you Lee! Now please don't get me wrong. I am not telling you what to do. That is your free will decision. And I am not trying to guilt you into not buying your dream car. What I am trying to do is help you see the big picture and identify any possible obstacles down the road that might cause you to veer away from my predestined will for you Lee; I don't want anything to damage or destroy our relationship or your relationship with others. Does that make sense?

Lee: Yes sir, it does. It's like what I have or don't have, what I do or don't do, what I say or don't say is my decision. That's my free will.

God: Yes sir.

Lee: What I need to do is make sure my free will decisions do not get in the way of my relationship with you or with others; That my will, does not cause me to violate your will; That my will, will not damage or destroy my connection with you and with others. That your will be done on earth, as it is in heaven.

God: I think you have answered your own question, Lee.

Lee: Yes sir, I think I have.

God: You have any more questions for me?

Lee: I will always have questions for you Lord.

God: I certainly hope so!

As we bring our Will of God journey to a close, based on what we have encountered along our journey, I would like for you to give serious consideration to the proposition, that rather than it being a question of God's will verses our will, it should be how does our will measure up to God's will.

This doesn't just apply to buying an $82,000.00 BMW! Measuring our will up to God's will should be the first step in answering questions we have about anything. Measuring our will up to God's will should be the first step in making decisions about anything.

That first step may be as simple as asking yourself a few questions:

1. Does what I have or don't have, what I do or don't do, or what I say or don't say get in the way of my relationship with God or with others?
2. Is my will causing me to violate God's will?
3. Does my will have the potential to damage or destroy my connection with God and with others?
4. When I pray, thy will be done on earth, as it is in heaven, am I telling the truth, the whole truth, and nothing but the truth, so help me God?

It seems to me that in the final analysis, the only person that can answer those questions is you! It is my hope and prayer that the thoughts and insights I have shared with you will in some way help you to answer what the Will of God is for you.

References

[1] Bronson, Michael. *Finding the Elusive Will of God.* E-Book: www.biblehelp.org, 1984.

[2] Clinton, Hilary Rodham. *It Takes A Village and Other Lessons Children Teach Us.* New York: Simon & Shuster, 1996.

[3] Cheney, Lois A. *God is No Fool.* Abingdon Press, 1969.

Nelson's Illustrated Bible Dictionary. 1986, Thomas Nelson Publishers, Nashville, TN 37214.

Unless otherwise indicated, all scripture quotations are taken from the *Holy Bible*, New International Version (NIV)

Scripture quotations marked (NLT) are taken from the *Holy Bible*, New Living Translation: 1996. Tyndale House Publishers, Inc., Wheaton, Illinois 60189.

Scripture quotations marked (KJV) are taken from the *Holy Bible*, King James Version.

Scripture quotations marked (NKJV) are taken from the *Holy Bible*, New King James Version.

Scripture quotations marked (NRSV) are taken from the *Holy Bible*, New Revised Standard Version.

Scripture quotations marked (MSG) are taken from the *Holy Bible*, Message: The Bible in Contemporary Language, by Eugene H. Peterson: 1993. NavPress Publishing Group, Colorado Springs, CO.

CPSIA information can be obtained
at www.ICGtesting.com
Printed in the USA
FFOW02n1906250214
3865FF